E.D. Burns has taken a massive cessible to missionary practiti discerning laypersons. *The Transcultural Gospel* cuts through the haze of subjectivity in modern missions and presses the non-negotiables of the gospel. In an age where lived experience sits enthroned, this book will restore your delight in gospel truth. And best of all, Burns provides interviews and sample questions for pre-evangelism that will help you to put what you're learning into practice as you make disciples. Read this book and give it to every missionary you know.

– Alex Kocman | Director of Advancement
and Communications, ABWE

Having recently read E.D. Burns' excellent book *The Missionary-Theologian*, I was delighted to hear about his newest work, *The Transcultural Gospel*, and could not wait to immerse myself into it too. The Great Commission is a spoken mission on a global scale. This commission's target is the ethnicities of the world, and its message is the contents of all that Jesus taught and incorporates in the sixty-six books of the Bible. Through hard charging yet graceful reasoning, Burns engages readers, regardless of their culture, to conclude that the only way to change the world is by making disciples— men and women who will delight in living for God's glory alone with, by, and through the timeless-boundless inerrant Word of God. This, too, is the heartbeat of The Master's Academy International, which is to train indigenous church leaders to be approved pastor-teachers, able to equip their churches to make biblically sound disciples. It is for these reasons that I commend to you *The Transcultural Gospel*.

– Dr. Eric Weathers | Senior Vice President, Strategic Partnerships,
The Master's Academy International

In this short and practical book, Burns rightly places contextualization in missions and evangelism within Scriptural bounds by defending the transcultural truth of God's Word while showing the ways that Scripture itself applies the gospel to the world's value systems.

– Seth Vitrano-Wilson | Director of Biblical Translation
for the Middle East Center for World Missions,
Horizons International

E.D. Burns has written a helpful and timely defense of why the Protestant gospel does not need to be changed in order to be received by every tribe, tongue, and nation. Contemporary notions of cultural contextualization have made the gospel into a wax nose that is reshaped to suit the felt needs of a particular people group. Burns understands that even if a missionary or an angel preaches a gospel contrary to what we received in God's transcultural Word, then he is anathema. What you have in your hands is a faithful guide through the shifting sands of sociology and cultural anthropology, which dominate contemporary missiology, and back to the sure bedrock of Scripture alone.

– Chad Vegas | Senior Pastor of Sovereign Grace Church and
Founding Board Chairman of Radius International

Missions today is loaded with "silver bullet" methodologies that promise much but deliver little. This practical little book reminds us that the clear teaching of the gospel is relevant and powerful throughout the ages and throughout human culture. Aspiring missionaries and pastors will be greatly helped by this book in thinking through the complex issue of contextualization and its implications in cross-cultural ministry.

– Brooks Buser | President, Radius International

In an increasingly connected and globally minded world, it is imperative that Christians have a growing fluency in a transcultural gospel. Not only are we sending missionaries to the world but on a daily basis the world is coming to us. As Christians, we are called to engage those who come into our lives as missionaries, whatever field we find ourselves in. Dr. Burns' book is a field manual for every Christian to understand, formulate, and engage a plan for missions/evangelism that is thoroughly biblical and imminently useful among all people groups the world over. It slices through the confusion of many unique cultural challenges and gets to the heart of the saving Good News and sufficiency of Jesus Christ. As a pastor I find this work to be an invaluable tool to equip the church that I serve, encourage the missionaries we support, and deploy for screening future candidates for ministry and missions. Christians who desire a faithful and thoroughly biblical understanding of presenting the gospel the world over will be blessed by this work.

– Dr. Brian Fairchild | Pastor, Colonial Bible Church, Midland, Texas

I am taken by the writing of Dr. Burns. He has the mind of a theologically astute missiologist and the heart of a biblically informed missionary, and he expresses himself winsomely and with precision and clarity. In The Transcultural Gospel, Burns helps us differentiate between primary and secondary gospel paradigms as they relate to all the world's cultures and values. This feat is not as easy as it may seem. The church is awash with soft evangelicalism that seems to be replacing robust biblical Christianity. And many of the church's global missions endeavors have suffered mission drift by way of hyper-contextualization, often to the point of diminishing essential doctrines and robbing the gospel of its God-given, Christ-honoring offensiveness. Burns points us to the classic doctrines of Scripture as the unchanging, not-to-be-diminished, core of the transcultural gospel, relevant for all cultures and central for all value systems. He does this in a way that is accessible and that exudes a deep passion and keen concern for God's global glory. I plan to make this book required reading in my circles of positional influence, and I will strongly recommend it in my circles of personal influence. It's that good.

João Mordomo, D.Int.St., PhD | Co-founder and Vice-Chair,
Crossover Global Catalyst (Senior Associate), Lausanne Movement
Professor of Missiology and Intercultural Studies

If you are thinking and praying about going to the mission field, wait! Do not go until you have read this book! Having been born overseas as a third-generation missionary still living on the field and now working to equip pastors and leaders from all around the world, I can tell you that we do not want a "contextualized" gospel approach to missions. We want a Word-centered, gospel-driven reformation that shamelessly upholds the ancient gospel. This small treasure will help you think through this topic very carefully and better prepare you for what God has entrusted to you.

Rick Denham, | 9Marks International Director,
Desiring God Global Spreading Manager,
and International Director for Editora FIEL.

THE *Transcultural* GOSPEL

E.D. BURNS

FOUNDERS
MINISTRIES
CAPE CORAL, FLORIDA

The Transcultural Gospel: Jesus Is Enough for Sinners in Cultures of Shame, Fear, Bondage, and Weakness

©2021 Founders Press

Published by
Founders Press

P.O. Box 150931 • Cape Coral, FL • 33915
Phone: (888) 525-1689
Electronic Mail: officeadmin@founders.org
Website: www.founders.org

Printed in the United States of America

ISBN: 978-1-943539-26-0

Cover Design by Jaye Bird LLC

Interior Design by InkSmith Editorial Services

Contents

For Elijah and Isaiah,
arrows in the hands of a warrior.

Fight the good fight.
Finish the race.
Keep the faith.

Hope in Christ.

*Faith and grace are the terms of
exchange between Man and God.
To have faith is to fix our eyes on Jesus.*
— John Sung Shang Chieh, 宋尚节

*The center of the Bible, and the center of Christianity, is
found in the grace of God; and the necessary corollary of
the grace of God is salvation through faith alone.*
— J. Gresham Machen

*But when the goodness and loving kindness of God our
Savior appeared, He saved us, not because of works done
by us in righteousness, but according to his own mercy, by
the washing of regeneration and renewal of the Holy Spirit,
whom He poured out on us richly through Jesus Christ
our Savior, so that being justified by His grace we might
become heirs according to the hope of eternal life.*
— Titus 3:4–7

Foreword

The cultural context in which this book is written is one that I breathe every day. So, as I write this foreword, I am not trying to imagine life in such a context. This is life for me. What I find exciting about this book is that it expresses what I have often wanted to have stated unambiguously; namely, that the gospel of Christ as taught in the Word of God is enough in every culture. Christ is enough in a shame and honor culture as He is enough in any other culture. Only as those who preach God's Word and counsel individual Christians see this truth will the church be a beacon of hope for our world.

Those who are called by God to minister in a context that is not their natural habitat should ingest the contents of this book. I have in mind missionaries who leave a Western culture to minister in, say, an African or Asian culture. They need to read a book like this because culture is a blind spot. Unless you try to understand the culture in which you are called to minister, you often end up being like a round peg in a square hole without even realizing it. You wonder why you are so ineffective in your efforts to evangelize the local people and to build them up in their most holy faith. It is because you do not really know how to scratch where it is itching with the gospel of the Lord Jesus Christ.

"A bad carpenter blames his tools" is an adage many of us are familiar with. What we do not realize is that its message desperately needs heeding by those of us who minister God's Word today. Anthropologists and other social scientists give the impression that different cultures need a different message altogether and that unless the church realizes this, it will be ineffective and irrelevant. Therefore, it needs to be stated once again that the good old gospel of the Lord Jesus is the tool that all Christian preachers and teachers need today as much as in the days of the apostles. It is the same message that needs to address the deepest needs of human hearts in every culture across the globe. If we think it is failing, it is most likely because we are bad carpenters. Burns helps us to take a second look at how we are using the tool of the gospel. As you read this book you soon discover that it is your method that needs to be corrected rather than the gospel. The gospel of Christ is transcultural. Do not try to chop of any of its edges to fit any culture.

All human beings are made in the image of God. All human beings inherited a fallen nature from Adam and Eve. All human beings came under the curse of God that was pronounced upon Adam and Eve in the garden of Eden. These stubborn facts transcend all cultures. Therefore, the greatest need for all human beings in every culture is how to be reconciled to God. Only after that should we ever hope that there can be any reconciliation to one another and to our environment. Thankfully, in the gospel of the Lord Jesus Christ, we have a very clear message. Paul puts it succinctly when he says, "In Christ God was reconciling the world to himself, not counting their trespasses against them, and entrusting to us the message of reconciliation" (2 Corinthians 5:19). This was through the substitutionary atoning death of Christ on the cross. Everything else flows from there. This must be taught to all people in every generation. It is a transcultural message.

Many books are either academic or practical. There are very few that manage to span this divide. This book by E.D. Burns manages to do both. This is because the author has labored in the classroom and at the same time lived in a foreign culture in which he seeks to apply the gospel. He is writing from experience and from a mind that has wrestled with how to communicate these truths to those who must teach others also. Thus, you have a book you can use in the classroom to prepare pastors and missionaries or use in the church to disciple young believers. Burns refers to a book he has written that is more academic than this, but trust me, this is a great primer!

— Conrad Mbewe

Preface

This book is the product of many years of teaching, conversations, and study. Much of this book derives from discussions and lectures on fear/peace, shame/honor, guilt/righteousness, weakness/strength, and bondage/freedom that I have been giving for years throughout the Middle East, Asia, and Africa. Based on those lectures, I intentionally created this book to be user-friendly for missionaries and practitioners. It does not say everything I wish to say, nor does it footnote and evidence my years of study and missions practice.

The introduction outlines this book's background, main ideas, and goals. Chapter 1 briefly surveys the centrality of the Bible and basic doctrines that missionaries should consider when thinking through how to explain the gospel cross-culturally. Chapter 2 highlights and unpacks the centrality of Christ's penal substitutionary atonement and righteousness and our response of faith alone. It argues for the centrality of a guilt/righteousness paradigm for all other cultural value systems. Chapter 3 discusses how to apply a guilt/righteousness paradigm to shame/honor contexts. Chapter 4 takes the same paradigm and applies it to fear/peace value systems. Chapter 5 considers it in bondage/freedom value systems. Chapter 6 applies the guilt/righteousness paradigm to weakness/ strength value systems. Finally, the conclusion rehearses and illustrates the big ideas of the transcultural gospel model.

After putting this book together, I realized a more academically corroborated and theologically expanded volume was necessary. I make many assertions and applications in this short book that do not require footnotes or sources. However, to make a persuasive case with thorough research, I have written a companion edition called *Ancient Gospel, Brave New World: Jesus Still Saves Sinners in Cultures of Shame, Fear, Bondage, and Weakness.* My suggestion would be to read this practical book first, consider how to apply its theological truths to your ministry, and then when you want in-depth details, read that longer academic edition. There might appear to be some occasional repetition between the two editions. But I created them to say the same essential things. The longer volume is more comprehensive (to be convincing), and this one is much more applicational (to be concrete). Both employ a similar persuasive and devotional style.

Acknowledgments

I am grateful to my students who first urged me to write this short book. Through many discussions about this book's ideas and on various occasions, Patrick Schreiner, Ryan Lister, and Josh Mathews of Western Seminary all encouraged me to put this together. I am also honored and privileged to enjoy friendship with so many missionaries and pastors all around the world who love the gospel, proclaim the truth, and carry a like-minded burden to take the gospel of Christ to the unreached and undiscipled.

I am grateful to my friends Rick Holland, Mike Abendroth, Vern Poythress, James Dolezal, Chad Vegas, Brooks Buser, Chris Martin, Alex Kocman, Ahshuwah Hawthorne, and Tanner Heath, who provided helpful feedback after reviewing the basic ideas and framework of this book. Also, I wish to thank Tanner Heath and Atalie Snyder, who both kindly helped me create a digital copy of my hand-drawn sketch of "The Transcultural Gospel Model." And I am thankful for the colleagues, friends, pastors, students, and ministry partners who encourage my teaching, writing, and translation, some of whom I have included in my acknowledgments in *Ancient Gospel, Brave New World*. God has blessed me with so many like-minded brothers and sisters that I cannot even list them all.

My stronghearted father, my faithful mother, my joyful sister, my sacrificial, lovely wife, my God-fearing sons, my supportive pastors/elders, my ministry partners, and my co-laborers in the Great Commission—all are God's gifts to me. They are those unknown, silent saints in the land, of whom the world is not worthy.

I wish to thank the faculties at Western Seminary and Asia Biblical Theological Seminary for encouraging me to write and produce the best materials I can for our students and for the nations. I admire and respect both Chuck Conniry at Western and Jim Blumenstock at ABTS. I truly feel humbled to teach and serve under their leadership. I'm grateful to Mike Sidders for believing in me and giving me time to write this book. And one of the humblest men I know, Dave Bennett has always prayed for me and encouraged my theological and missiological leadership, for which I am indebted. Ben Mosier has been the friend who sticks closer than a brother since we were young kids, and I am grateful to God for him. Finally, to my wife, who provided a writing leave in 2019 for me to first launch this project, and to my sons, who are so encouraging of my writing ministry: I love you always and forever.

Above all else, the sovereign grace of the triune God is beyond description and without rival. Thank you, my Lord, for saving even me, in Christ alone, by grace alone, through faith alone.

E.D. Burns
Thailand
December 2019

Introduction

During the sixteenth century, German monk Martin Luther (1483–1546) stood against the authority of the Church of Rome and the pope by elevating the Word of Christ above every other authority. The Roman Catholic Church viewed itself as determinative over the Bible and its message. It was Luther's rediscovery of the centrality of Christ's righteousness in the written Word that launched a gospel reformation and revival throughout Europe and essentially threw off the shackles of Rome's control over the Word of God.

Similarly, the global evangelical church of the twenty-first century has seemingly slipped into a self-made trap of heeding popular social ideas to interpret and apply Scripture relevantly and respectably. As Christians once languished under the theological captivity of popes and councils, so we now also struggle under the pressure of our cultural captivity. We grow weary of aping the latest talking points, attempting to make the gospel fit every cultural nuance, and relinquishing theological priority and prominence to each person's unique standpoint. These are not merely neutral cultural communication techniques for contextualizing the gospel. This repackaging of the gospel based on identity, intersectionality, and standpoint is the effect of a brave new religion. It blurs the transcultural distinctiveness of the faith once for all delivered to the saints.

The spirit of the age has profoundly permeated our sensibilities. It seems narrow-minded and unsophisticated to suggest that the controlling framework of our theology and missiology should be the self-interpreting Word and its historical gospel doctrines. Instead, indicative of secular theology, we readily query the culture's ecumenical priorities and multi-perspectival value systems to relevantly adapt the gospel. And this tendency is likely no more evident than in contemporary global missions. We desperately need a Word-centered, doctrine-driven reformation that shamelessly upholds the ancient gospel for missions. We must recover the ancient gospel. Its transcultural truths will outlast the brave new religion of this brave new world.

Cultural Captivity

Is truth dynamic or static? Does objective truth even matter anymore? Does a transcendent standard for interpreting reality still exist? Or is our relationship to reality so subjective that our "lived experience" is our only authoritative framework? Instead of living in a postmodern era of creative liberation, increasingly it seems that the globalized culture is plunging into a post-truth dark age. A problem with the popular culture's disdain for objective truth and suspicion of all external authority is that it influences even how Christian scholarship seeks to answer society's questions. To retain "influence" and "engage the culture" with a "brave prophetic voice," some Christian leaders inevitably adapt their methods to appear accommodating and open-minded. Then, after they have surrendered authoritative proclamation for "robust conversation" and "winsome discourse," their message slowly softens. They then find themselves neglecting or even abandoning core historical evangelical doctrines altogether. This is quickly becoming an obvious threat in the broader Christian world.

To the surprise of many, this tendency toward soft evangelicalism and cultural captivity has been quite common on the mission field for decades. Methods of hyper-contextualization have so universally permeated missions training and agencies that many missionaries consider the historical Christian doctrines to be impractical cargo to be jettisoned in the name of efficiency, effectiveness, political correctness, social acceptability, and cultural sensitivity. Because of this tendency to over-contextualize and minimize doctrine, the true gospel as the Holy Spirit has illumined it throughout the ages can fade into the background of other expressions and emphases of culturally nuanced gospels.

The Aim of This Book

The main point of this book is to provide a helpful model for how the historical "great exchange" of the gospel—Christ's substitutionary death and imputed righteousness—relates to some of the world's macro-cultural orientations and their corresponding value systems. As I mentioned in the preface, this book is an abbreviated and practical version of a longer, in-depth volume: *Ancient Gospel, Brave New World: Jesus Still Saves Sinners in Cultures of Shame, Fear, Bondage, and Weakness.*[1] Because that book grew out of this initial project, I state some similar and identical concepts in both, though considerably more expounded and supported in the other. Some applicational content is unique to this one, and overall, the other edition is much more content heavy. To illustrate content, *Ancient Gospel, Brave New World* employs some extra anecdotes, character conversations, and real-life examples that this edition does not. I intended this book to be helpful and useful for practitioners, whereas I designed the other edition to be substantial and persuasive. Though this is a practitioner-level book, both volumes maintain an identical thesis:

---

1   Cape Coral, FL: Founders Press, 2021.

Many cultures value honor, peace, freedom, and strength, and the way the world achieves them requires doing enough according to a common code. But Christian doctrine teaches that Christ's substitutionary work is sufficient to secure such blessings and benefits. They are benefits of the gospel that God bestows freely on the legal ground of Christ's imputed righteousness. And so, united to Christ through faith alone, we receive Christ and all that He is for us—infinite, immutable, and eternal honor, peace, freedom, and strength. God's ways are not man's ways.

This book argues that the centrality of a guilt/righteousness paradigm is the standard key to unlocking the gospel for the world's macro cultural value paradigms of shame/honor, fear/peace, bondage/freedom, and weakness/strength. Trust alone receives Christ Himself and His benefits/blessings secured by His righteousness and atonement. Those gospel benefits/blessings are the true substance of the patterns of God's image valued in some cultural orientations. The exchanges of Christ's righteousness and His benefits/blessings for our unrighteousness and curse depend on His substitution and imputation.

The biblical gospel neither adapts nor adopts the imperfect meaning of the world's value systems. Rather, with transcendent truth, the Bible reinterprets and fills up what is biblically defined as honor, peace, freedom, and strength, bringing clarity to them in the light of the lordship of Christ. The transcultural Word of God brings cohesion and meaning to those cultural value systems by showing how the benefits/blessings of Christ's work depend on the redemptive center of His work: penal substitutionary atonement, the imputation of His righteousness, adoption into His family, reconciliation with God, and union with Him in His death and resurrection.

The curse-tainted image of God in cultural value systems esteems the true, good, and beautiful aspects of honor, peace, freedom, and strength. Learning how cultures interpret reality and prioritize value systems is important for steering people toward the gospel's solution to the original sin problem. And learning how cultures contextually interpret ideas and value systems is helpful for knowing how to disciple someone to conform their thinking to the eternal gospel.

To put it another way, because of those aforementioned essential salvation doctrines that have consistently dominated the Spirit's illumining work throughout church history, sinners who rest in Christ alone can freely enjoy the grace-filled benefits/ blessings of His active and passive obedience. These blessings include the exchange of our shame, fear, bondage, and weakness for His honor, peace, freedom, and strength—the expiation of our shameful, fearmongering, enslaving, and impoverishing *guilt* for the imputation of Christ's honorable, peace-giving, liberating, and strengthening *righteousness*.

This book is not a duplication of the popular works on shame/ honor, fear/power, and guilt/innocence. Rather, it adapts those themes as *dependent* on the classic doctrines of the gospel, specifically those recovered by the Reformation. This book applies the biblical gospel as the center that holds together all these popular paradigms and value systems.[2]

Having evaluated some of the widely accepted value systems, such as fear/power and guilt/innocence, I believe the biblical evidence doesn't fully support those pairs. I have reframed them as fear/peace and guilt/righteousness and have prioritized guilt/ righteousness as *central* to the other pairs, from which they all emanate. Also, I have coined pairs of values systems (e.g., bondage/freedom and weakness/strength) based on biblical evidence that I perceive fits within their respective cultural orientations, which I elaborate and illustrate.

---

2 See "The Transcultural Gospel Model" and "The Transcultural Gospel Model and Overlapping Value Systems" in the appendixes.

There could be other cultural value systems. But in terms of macro-level cultural orientations and value systems, the four offered in this book seem to represent most societies and cultures, complement each other well, and overlap quite naturally. They make sense of the big-picture gospel blessings/benefits granted to us in Christ. By basic observation, some of these value systems might interrelate so much that they seem more similar than different. That's a fair observation. Nevertheless, people in each value system prioritize differently their version of the fundamental problem, their corresponding solution, and their rules to do enough to get blessings.

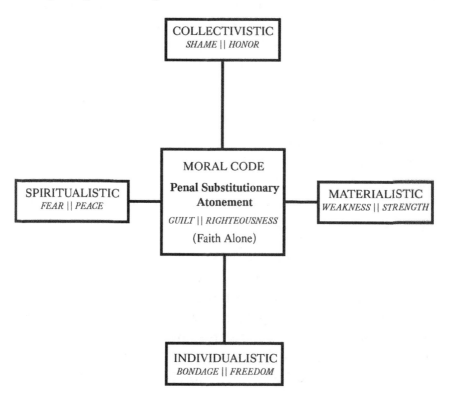

For convenience and clarity, included below is the "The Transcultural Gospel Model" from the appendix. This is the model I use for this book:

How to Use This Book

Preparation: Questions to Ask Your Target Culture

There are many questions to ask in pre-evangelism and in discipleship. For example, pre-evangelism questions should include topics such as these: creation (origins, ancestors, evidence of the curse, etc.), God (who, where, what, etc.), good/bad (examples, source, etc.), and death (where, why, what). The point is to create a tension in the unbeliever's interpretation of reality and existence. We want them to doubt the source and authority of their belief and value system. Moreover, we need to ask them to define terms and explain what they mean. A useful concept to remember is that *clarity is the enemy of error*. Probing the person's source, authority, and definition helps bring clarity to confusion and falsehood. Be sure to also ask these questions: What do you mean by that? Why do you believe that? How do you know? Who told you? How do they know?

We must expose that they don't have all the answers and that even some of their answers are dissatisfying. But before immediately providing a brief gospel explanation, it is wiser to delay it and tell them that the Bible answers these questions. Inform the person you will provide teaching on a later date (with other interested locals) to explain what the Bible says about these questions. Read this book with these example questions in mind about the people in your target culture:

1. What are their good, true, and beautiful cultural value systems that seem to pattern the image of God? What are their virtues and vices? What is their conscious cultural

orientation? What could be other cultural values and orientations through which they view reality but might not consciously realize?

2. How might you discern the transcendent themes they value most (honor, peace, freedom, strength, etc.)?

3. What is the solution they seek in life? How does that reveal their perceived problem?

4. What do they do to achieve that solution?

5. When do they know they have done enough? How?

6. Why do they believe this? Who or what is their authority?

7. In what ways and to what extent can you teach them about mankind's original sin problem in Adam and its effects on all cultural value systems?

8. How can you help them see Christ as the Last Adam?

9. How can you guide them to understand Christ's great exchange on the cross?

10. How can you help them understand repentance and faith alone in Jesus the Savior-King?

Listen for their "solutions" to repair and remedy what they perceive is not right in their lives. In so doing, you might be able to locate their solution (enough merit, enough loyalty, enough ritual, enough sincerity, etc.) to their perceived original problem (as they understand it according to their moral code). Listen for language of "enoughness." Ask, "When do you know it's enough?" Also, one way to identify the accepted idol of a culture is to probe what kind of speech and terminology they forbid. Every culture has blasphemy laws, and if you can discover what they consider blasphemous, you might be able to trace it to what they treasure most. They usually despise the words and ideas they forbid, so be careful not to unnecessarily give offense. The gospel is offensive, but we don't want to be in our probing or behavior.

Reflection: Questions to Ask Yourself

When you are in the process of pre-evangelism question-asking and when you are seeking to disciple someone in the target culture, consider asking yourself questions like these:

1. Am I praying from start to finish for their eyes to be opened to wonderful things in God's law, for the miracles of regeneration and sanctification?

2. How can I help these people understand the main message of Scripture?

3. Have I carefully explained the inerrancy, sufficiency, and authority of God's Word? Have I shown how it transcends all generations and all ethnolinguistic cultures?

4. Have I helped these people see how the effects of the curse of which they are experientially aware (shame, fear, bondage, weakness, etc.) relate to mankind's original sin problem: guilt and corruption in Adam?

5. Have I miscommunicated the gospel in any way that might lead these people to trust in a combination of doing enough in addition to grace?

6. What are the potential counterfeit gospels these people might be prone to believe, and how can I help warn against them?

7. Have I communicated the gospel in a way that these people see how the "great exchange" of Christ's work on their behalf is His penal substitutionary atonement and imputation of righteousness?

8. How can I help them understand how Christ's benefits and blessings of honor, peace, freedom, and strength flow from the sufficiency of His work?

9. Are they trusting in and deriving assurance from their loyalty and submission to Christ, or are they resting in Christ alone?

10. How can I help them trust in Christ as Savior and King in a way that they rest in His kingly power and authority to save them?

Final Comments

This book, just as the other edition, will have its limitations and blind spots. They are all my own. What I articulate and explain at this stage in my Christian life, theological development, and missionary calling will hopefully all grow and sharpen over time. Even as I have studied and written this book's contents over the years, I have self-corrected and discovered personal, theological, and missiological deficiencies. Instead of waiting to publish this until I have "arrived" and "got it all figured out" (which is not possible in this life), I decided to ask some friends and colleagues (mentioned in the acknowledgments) to give me feedback and to help me locate areas for improvement. I assume that even after publishing this, I will regret saying something the way I did or excluding something I wish I would have said. That sense of personal disappointment with the final product is normal for anyone who serves the Lord—pastors wishing they could have preached their sermons better, missionaries wishing they could have mastered the language better, counselors wishing they would have said something else, and parents regretting not being encouraging enough while their kids were still around. This reason—that we can never do well enough—motivated me to write this book. From start to finish, no matter our cultural and ethnolinguistic background and irrespective of our Christian service, God's grace in Christ is enough for us, and we receive those blessings in Christ as we trust in Him alone.

My prayer is that this short book will be helpful in preparing for pre-evangelism, evangelism, and discipleship. I do not intend to answer most questions about transferrable theological distinctives/traditions and degrees of contextualization, techniques, communication styles, and other methodological issues. My aim is to simply help the reader think through how to lead a conversation using the perceived cultural values of a people to move the discussion naturally and cogently to the gospel solution of Christ's substitutionary atonement and imputation of righteousness as it satisfies the problem of original sin and condemnation in Adam. And all the benefits and blessings of union with Christ because of His passive and active obedience are received and enjoyed through trust alone, in Christ alone, by grace alone, to the glory of God alone, revealed in Scripture alone. *Post tenebras lux.*

> *By awesome deeds You answer us in righteousness,.*
> *O God of our salvation,*
> *You who are the trust of all the ends of the earth*
> *and of the farthest sea.*
> – Psalm 65:5 NASB95

CHAPTER 1

Christ's Word
over Culture

What does the gospel according to the Chinese have in common with the gospel according to the Cherokee? Or the gospel according to the Basque gypsies and the gospel according to the Aboriginals? You might observe that none of these ethnolinguistic groups come from traditionally Western backgrounds. And the conclusion might be that since they all likely operate in a collectivistic orientation and determine value through a shame/honor paradigm, then their interpretive methods and self-theologized teachings should be thoroughly "non-Western."

In other words, they have escaped many of the trappings of Greco/Roman philosophical categories, medieval legal constructs, European rationalism, and American individualism. The reasoning goes, such contemporary Eastern cultures, though separated by millennia (also by language and geography) from the cultures of the ancient Near East (ANE), are poised better than their Western counterparts to discover the true heart of the Bible's relational narrative. Such a community-oriented, justice-advancing, and relationally dynamic approach to the gospel seems to diverge significantly from any gospel message that entails law, righteousness, atonement, and propitiation. This is an increasingly popular opinion in missions. Many believe that Martin Luther explicated the gospel as he perceived it would best answer the questions he was asking as a hyper-conscientious, scrupulous monk whose early training to be a lawyer exacerbated his law-fixation. So, as Protestants, we are the cultural recipients of his guilt/innocence gospel paradigm.

Then, as some popularly propose, the challenge is to deconstruct and even de-colonize the gospel from its Western legal interpretations so other cultural value systems can discover and define the gospel for their cultural value system. The triune God then becomes a missionary who adapts and adopts various cultural priorities in order to contextualize the gospel in symbols, images, and ideas they understand and value. Essentially, God is in process, progressively revealing Himself as history unfolds and as different cultures have the opportunity to self-theologize the gospel. The Bible becomes a living constitution, as it were, that different cultures can interpret dynamically depending on their standpoint. Some see reality through a shame/honor lens, while fear and power influence others. Each group has its own perspective and unique way of approximating truth.

These assertions are not uncommon in global missions influenced by modernist, historicist, Biblicist, and progressive ideas. Though they might sound charitably multi-perspectival and liberally multicultural, they are ironically Western and postmodern. Words have meaning, and theological ideas have eternal consequences.

How do we make sense of these frequent attempts to undermine biblical authority, historical doctrines, theological accuracy, and gospel specificity? This is especially a challenge in missions because missionaries and missiologists are often the tip of the proverbial spear when it comes to innovative methods, creative theology, and novel contextualization. Moreover, one reason why such theological innovations go unnoticed in missions is that few missionaries have undergone sufficient training in classic Christian doctrine, historical theology, biblical languages, and systematic theology. Consequently, few can rightly divide the Word, hold fast to historic doctrinal essentials, and discern old-fashioned error that has already been defeated in previous generations. To be sure, not every missionary needs an equal amount of training. On one end, some might serve in a deacon-like role as support staff, while on the other end, others might serve in an elder-like role as church planters and Bible translators.

Nonetheless, to help people understand why the gospel is *good* news, knowing a few fundamental categories as a background is of immense significance and essential value: the centrality and perspicuity of the Bible, the effects of the original sin problem, how cultures are fallen and are unable to recover the good, true, and beautiful virtues of God's image. Then, after surveying these, in the proceeding chapters, we can explore how the work of Christ is enough to secure our righteousness and all the derivative honorable, peaceful, liberating, and strengthening benefits/ blessings of our union with Him.

God's Culture-Transcending Word

A missionary who is mainly seeking to *relevantly contextualize* the gospel might unintentionally change the gospel to fit it within the target cultural value system. But a missionary who is mainly seeking to *rightly communicate* the gospel will seek to understand the culture's value system and language so he can clearly explain the original problem of guilt and corruption in Adam and the corresponding solution of Christ's penal substitutionary atonement and imputed righteousness. Such a missionary will then show

how Christ secures the good, true, and beautiful aspects of that culture's perceived values for those who receive Christ through faith alone.

Sometimes the missionary, in an early conversation, must lead with the target people's categories to get to the gospel, but that is not always the case. And often a missionary must prioritize the principal thing to emphasize in the moment—potentially a disagreeable definition of terms or a kindhearted conversation that creates opportunities for follow-up meetings and gospel teaching.

The Bible alone is alive, active, sufficient, inerrant, and authoritative, and transcendent over every other human writing, idea, or value system, even if they resemble God's common grace and reflect shades of the pre-fallen image of God. Despite any ultimate purpose they might serve in God's sovereignty, they must come under the lordship of Christ and find true meaning and definition in light of His revealed Word.

To rightly divide the Word of truth and to avoid the modernist errors of historicism (exegeting the historical events and original cultures), cultural gnosticism (discovering spiritual knowledge through the lens of the original audience), and standpoint theory (interpreting Scripture through the particular cultural and existential standpoints of typically the marginalized), we must first understand basic truths about the Author's (capital *A*) inspiration of the biblical text. The Holy Spirit's inspiration of the Word indeed uses common ANE cultural-linguistic expressions. In other words, the Holy Spirit doesn't speak some extraterrestrial language foreign to the audience. Nevertheless, the Holy Spirit is not *restricted* to ANE cultural-linguistic expressions. The Spirit at Pentecost essentially reversed Babel, and all the various language groups heard identical timeless truth and a transcultural message of the magnificence of God's saving power, yet in their own tongue:

> And how is it that we hear, each of us in his own native language? Parthians and Medes and Elamites and residents of Mesopotamia, Judea and Cappadocia, Pontus and Asia, Phrygia and Pamphylia, Egypt and the parts of Libya belonging to Cyrene, and visitors from Rome, both Jews and proselytes, Cretans and Arabians—we hear them telling in our own tongues the mighty works of God. (Acts 2:8–11)

A focus on divine authorial intent does not nullify the human authors. The issue is not either/or—choosing one over the other, human or divine authorial intent. It is typically a matter of *priority* and starting point in interpretive method and teaching. The reason this is relevant for missions is that when missionaries cross a culture and seek to contextualize the biblical message by giving priority to the human authors in order to bridge the "cultural meaning" gap to the target people, we inevitably misapply and even misconstrue the gospel. We look for connections and commonalities between our best guesses at ancient Near Eastern culture and our best perceptions of the target culture, as though communicating in and through their paradigms are of utmost importance. But if we start with looking for and heeding the self-interpreting and perspicuous divine authorial intent, we see the target culture as a fallen cultural orientation and value system that needs to be brought under the lordship of Christ. We can then evaluate it through the terms, categories, and priorities of the whole counsel of God. It's a matter of *theological* priority and focus. Divine authorial intent emphasizes that the Holy Spirit speaks *through* the human authors, often with future redemptive meanings beneath their cultural vocabulary that they didn't even grasp.

Heeding divine authorial intent pays attention to *what* (content) and *how* (structure) Scripture speaks. What is the proportionality of Scripture's emphasis? What is the final structure in which it fits together? Is Scripture mainly concerned with answering all our ethical questions, addressing the mysteries of the angelic realm, providing insights to success and upward mobility, or prescribing steps to freedom from addictions?

The sufficiency of the Bible directly relates to its divine design. It is reliably sufficient to achieve its God-breathed *telos*. Just as a commercial jet is designed and thus reliably sufficient to transport hundreds of passengers around the world due to its specialized design, it is not reliably sufficient to wage an air campaign on hostile enemy targets as would a fighter jet. Though they are both planes, a commercial airliner and a fighter jet are uniquely designed as sufficient for two distinct aims. Just as the intelligent design of creation is sufficient to inform us about the Creator, the *evangelical* design of Scripture is sufficient to convert and conform us to the Savior.

The Bible, under the sovereign authorship and canonization of the Spirit of Christ, indeed uses the idioms and linguistic nuances of the human writers, but it transcends their cultural conventions with a transcultural, transgenerational Christ-centered *telos*. The Bible sufficiently interprets itself, opening the door to paradise, as it were, turning on the hinge of Christocentrism (John 5:39–47; Luke 24:44–47). We must read the Scripture according to its own unique emphases, countercultural categories, and theological definitions as an interconnected composite whole. We must never let extrabiblical cultural value systems, as terminologically similar to Scripture as they might appear, presume precedence or even equivalence to the Bible's own terms and doctrinal definitions. In other words, the Bible uses words like *love*, *justice*, *power*, *honor*, *redemption*, and *blessing*. But their theological meaning qualitatively transcends any meaning a fallen culture might approximately apply to the same words.

To be sure, many biblical interpreters, missionaries, and teachers know how to define biblical terms with biblical meaning. We have lexicons and dictionaries and innumerable commentaries for such research. It's not uncommon to hear Bible teachers explain that commonly used words in English are not equally congruent with how the Bible uses them. For instance, the word *discipline* in common English often implies the correction or even punishment of a child, but the biblical and theological usage of the word *discipline* refers more to training and teaching. It is always rooted in God's filial love for His children and never implies penal retribution. Many Christians intuitively understand how to distinguish commonly used terms and definitions from biblically/theologically used terms and definitions. The point is not that most are oblivious to divine authorial intent and the theological definitions of biblical categories. Rather, the issue is that because we are so evangelistically concerned to connect and contextualize the gospel for target cultures—and justly so—we then prioritize what we perceive to be the similarities of the Bible's ANE cultural value systems and effectively underemphasize the transcendent divine *telos* of Scripture. And to be fair, this tendency is not for lack of evangelistic desire; it often stems from a lack of practice, awareness, or training.

What are the value systems of the target culture? How can we use their paradigms to explain the gospel? How do their paradigms help us understand the gospel outside our interpretive traditions? These are not uncommon missiological queries, and they are not bad questions. But we should beware of prioritizing such questions as though they were the only questions or even the main questions we should ask. Maybe a more penetrating question to ask would be "What solutions does their cultural paradigm propose in response to the convicted moral code of their conscience?" knowing that their solutions (merit, loyalty, ritual, sincerity, etc.) reveal their perceived problem. Once the perceived problem and proposed solution are located, then we can slowly explain how the benefits of Christ are secured and thus bestowed on the basis of Christ's penal substitutionary atonement (passive obedience) and imputed righteousness (active obedience), all to be received through faith alone.

Our Original Problem

Unless we delineate and reiterate the basics of sin (what it is and what it is not), our gospel solutions will seek to answer problems that are not fundamentally sin problems—social and religious feelings of shame, fear, bondage, weakness, and the like. They might indeed be implications and consequences of sin, and they might even be sinful in themselves. But they are not the original root problem.

The fundamental problem is that we are dead in sins, born guilty in Adam, and unable and unwilling to love God and love neighbor. Our gospel solutions reveal our perceived original problems. When missionaries forget the real sin problem, they spend themselves proposing new methods and even gospel doctrines to fix what is not foundationally broken. Is it bad that people suffer shame, fear, bondage, and weakness? Yes. But because these sin problems emerge from the original sin problem—guilt and condemnation in Adam—we then need to be united through faith to the Last Adam, covered by His penal substitutionary atonement, and imputed with His righteousness. When we confuse the effects of sin with its root problem, we confuse and pollute the simplicity of the gospel.

We are evil *at* the core. That is not to say that we are evil *to* the core, meaning we are not as evil as possible. The common grace in the image of God, marred as it might be in us, nevertheless remains intact. All humans can indeed do good in common grace—providing for one's family, throwing oneself onto a grenade, running into a burning building to save the helpless, adopting abused orphans, designing a dependable bridge with impeccable foundations—but such common-grace goodness is not truly righteous.

Natural Law and "Enoughness"

That all mankind is pervasively sinful is manifest in every culture, every age, and every individual. That the law of God is written on every heart in every cultural value system is apparent in the history of ancient civilizations and in anthropological observations of diverse people groups. That something deep down inside us all is pervasively wrong and tragically irreparable is also obvious.

Everyone intuitively knows they are not good enough, and no one truly knows the way back to Eden. But every cultural value paradigm that emerges from natural law proposes its own narrative detailing the original sin problem and then prescribes its own corresponding solution through believing, being, or doing enough. It's all about achieving "enoughness."

A moral code of natural law written on the heart of every individual in all ethnolinguistic groups serves as their ethical rudder, though bent and corrupted by the curse. That there is a general social order in all nations indicates the sway of a moral code from natural law on the hearts of men. And in the face of disorder and chaos, whether within a family or within a whole society, the law of God written on their hearts alerts them that it is wrong, bad, and evil.

The moral code inside all people pushes them to perform to attain enoughness—enough goodness, enough rightness, enough honor, enough peace, enough freedom, enough strength. On one end of the spectrum, in some cultural value systems that maintain a transcendent virtue of the remaining image of God, their pursuit of enoughness seems others-centered, anthropocentric, equitable, and humane—doing good to others to win honor, achieve peace, appear strong, and feel free. Conversely, on the opposite end of the spectrum, in other cultural value systems that have pervasively scorned transcendent virtue, their pursuit of enoughness looks commensurately self-centered, narcissistic, inequitable, and crude. They try doing enough to arrive at personal peace, gain popularity, live life to the full, and arrive at the destination of self-discovery and self-liberation. And this pursuit of a self-made moral code often treats other people as utilitarian; people are either an obstacle to overcome or an asset to use.

Gospel presentations according to proponents of fear/power value systems suggest that a broken code has plunged mankind into slavery to Satan. Gospel presentations according to proponents of shame/honor value systems suggest there is a code of honor that has been transgressed, resulting in consequent shame and abandonment. Though proponents of these value systems claim that guilt/innocence is its own unique value system of equal emphasis, Scripture seems to argue that, at the core, natural law influences every value system. And each system centers on the problem of original guilt. [1] For instance, fear and shame (and consequent bondage and weakness) emanate from the guilt of transgressing God's law, whether it be the code of a Gentile's conscience (see Romans 2:12–16) or the code of the Jewish law (Romans 2:17–27). The basis for fear and shame? The holy Creator and Judge. God's law is not an arbitrary list of rules. And God is not a mutable, capricious Allah, with unpredictable standards of righteousness and unrighteousness. God is orderly. God has a law. His law proceeds from His essence. To trespass, transgress, dishonor, and spurn God's objective law is to do the same to God Himself.

All Adam's descendants in every cultural value system intuitively know a code exists. If you have done something to dishonor your patron, and thus bring about shame, you have transgressed a moral code. You have trespassed a demarcation line—albeit maybe an imperfect cultural value. But it is still a breaking of a moral code that derives from the natural law imprinted on the heart. Doing or believing *this* is honorable, but doing or believing

---

1   See "The Transcultural Gospel Model" in appendix.

that is shameful. This, not that. There is a line, a boundary, a code. Cross the line. Trespass the boundary. Break the code. What is that called? Guilt. Shameful guilt, fearful guilt, enslaving guilt, weakening guilt. Guilt, nonetheless. You feel subjective shame because you are objectively guilty, just as Adam's fearful shame (Genesis 3:10) followed hard on the heels of his objective guilt and condemnation (Genesis 3:6). Shame is the emotive pain rooted in trespassing the conscience's moral code.

Every person knows deep down inside there is *individual* accountability before a holy God for how rightly we each walk according to the universal, natural law. That individual moral code operates on a God-given sense of rightness and wrongness, righteousness and guilt. And in these systems, the only hope for soothing a troubled conscience is enoughness. So they prescribe enough merits, loyalty, fealty, obedience, and compliance to the internal moral code. Everyone knows they are not righteous, but they do not know before whom they are guilty.

Church history demonstrates that swerving off-center is a perpetual threat. Adam's objective guilt imputed to us and our inherited inability to truly love God and others create an insurmountable problem for all humanity. To be sure, Christ dispenses benefits and blessings that correspond to our brokenness, weakness, bondage, shame, and other implications of sin and the curse. But the central work of Christ from which all the Spirit's blessings flow was giving us Himself, bringing us to the Father, as the *telos* of the gospel. And these blessings are only possible because of His resurrection after accomplishing penal substitutionary atonement and imputation of righteousness to guilty, unrighteous people.

Cultural Orientations and Cultural Value Systems

The missionary and missiologist must consider the nuances and possibilities of communicating the biblical gospel to a target culture without accommodating and fully adopting the cultural values themselves. To do this, understanding basic global cultural orientations and cultural value systems is vital. Moreover, evaluating them in light of God's standards is essential.

The overarching cultural orientations (i.e., individualistic/collectivistic and materialistic/spiritualistic) have a variation of cultural value systems/paradigms (i.e., shame/honor, fear/peace, bondage/freedom, and weakness/strength) through which peoples make value judgments. Moreover, these value systems and paradigms fit approximately—not exhaustively—within their larger cultural orientations.

These are the cultural orientations with their connected cultural value systems:

- COLLECTIVISTIC ORIENTATION
  - Shame/Honor Value System

- SPIRITUALISTIC ORIENTATION
  - Fear/Peace Value System

- INDIVIDUALISTIC ORIENTAITON
  - Bondage/Freedom Value System

- MATERIALISTIC ORIENTATION
  - Weakness/Strength Value System

Naturally, the lines between value systems and their common orientations are usually blurry. Their nuances depend on each ethnolinguistic people group's degree of emphasis on each cultural value. These orientations and paradigms all exist on a continuum with no cultural context fitting exclusively within a single orientation and system.

In approaching cultural orientations and value systems as *evangelical* missiologists and missionaries—not as sociological anthropologists—we must start with the heart of the gospel. And we must show how it might relate to the corresponding fallen *imago Dei* impulses of various cultural orientations and value systems/paradigms. Moreover, evangelical missiologists and missionaries must not argue for the blind redeeming of all cultures. No cultural orientation or value system is immune to the curse. All cultures are fallen, though not all fallen cultures are equal in degrees of wickedness. The Scripture affirms this by demonstrating that cultures diversely occupy the spectrum of conformity to God's natural law on one end to transgression of His law on the other end.

In common cultural orientations, their corresponding popular cultural value systems are often overanalyzed, overapplied, and uploaded into biblical systems and definitions. But this does not invalidate the usefulness of learning to understand such paradigms. Not to overstate the issue, these cultural value paradigms are indeed helpful. Any missionary-in-training would be a fool not to study them well for the sake of pre-evangelism conversations.

Positively, they are like salvation benefits emerging from the center of the gospel. Negatively, the curse touches each orientation and value system so that, left to themselves, they create counterfeit attempts at repairing what only the gospel of Christ can redeem. Each system as it stands alone should not be used to interpret the Bible. But the Bible in its own terms and doctrine should be the light that clarifies what each fallen cultural value system imperfectly approximates as good, true, and beautiful. Each cultural value system can be useful in pre-evangelism conversations to push people deeper to discover true solutions in gospel doctrine where their fallen value systems fall short to solve the original sin problem.

Remember to Think with the Mind of Christ

Through the written Word of Christ, the Spirit opens our eyes to see transcultural, virtuous truth and make sense of the enigmas of imperfect cultural paradigms that languish under the curse for lack of biblical clarity. The mind of Christ given to all believers in regeneration is an otherworldly, transcultural lens that enables us to peer through the fog of cursed cultural value systems. The more we set our minds on the written Word and seek to conform our thinking to biblical doctrine, the more we will discern how to rightly handle Scripture. We will accurately communicate the gospel to various cultural paradigms and compellingly identify those remaining visages of virtue in any cultural system.[2]

The unfolding of Your words gives light;
it imparts understanding to the simple.

— Psalm 119:130

---

2   To visualize how cultural value systems/paradigms fit within cultural orientations, see "The Transcultural Gospel Model" in appendix 1. For a visual that illustrates how the cultural value systems/paradigms overlap and influence one another, see appendix 2, "The Transcultural Gospel Model and Overlapping Value Systems."

CHAPTER 2

Christ
Our Righteousness

I sn't it culturally arrogant and insensitive to force our forensic view of salvation on people who do not interpret reality in the same way? Isn't that just the Western tradition's way of explaining the gospel? Isn't it merely a matter of cultural and interpretive emphasis?

These are common sentiments of missionaries and Christian leaders who have imbibed the West's progressive values of multiculturalism, political correctness, and cultural sensitivity training.

To be sure, learning the perspectives and cultural values of people outside traditional Western constructs is tremendously helpful and quite humbling at times. The traditions of the West are no closer to righteousness than other global traditions. Truly, the decadence and willful rejection in the West of God's revealed moral law is profoundly wickeder than any other fallen culture that has never had the opportunity to hear the gospel. The pre-Christian unreached have only had God's general revelation to reject, while some post-Christian apostates have rejected special revelation for generations. Judgment is coming hard and fast for the West.

Nevertheless, though Christian leaders codified classical evangelical doctrines in eras and countries that upheld traditional Greco-Roman, medieval, and Enlightenment legal systems, it does not mean that such gospel doctrines are *exclusively* products of their cultural systems. Rather, the creeds and the essential Trinitarian, Christological, and soteriological doctrines the Holy Spirit has illumined throughout church history serve as the doctrinal boundaries and guideposts for the universal church's system of beliefs. The classic gospel doctrines that employ forensic language—*substitution* and *imputation*—derive fundamentally not from the West but from the Jewish traditions and the Hebrew Scriptures themselves. The Jewish Christians, led by the Word of Christ, influenced the ancient church's confession that Christ's work for our salvation and its consequent blessings all grow out of His penal substitutionary atonement and imputed righteousness.

Human Wisdom vs. the Things of the Spirit

Someone might respond, "Okay, so I'll grant that this forensic language comes from Jewish influence and not the Western traditions only, but isn't that still an artifact of Jewish culture? What about other cultural artifacts from people in non-Jewish and non-Western contexts? What about their interpretive grids?"

The fact is that the Jews had millennia of building theology and culture around God's revealed Word. Though their interpretations often fell short of God's mysterious Messianic intentions, dwelling in the Hebrew Scriptures as the people of the Book influenced their value system more than any other surrounding culture. In reality, much of their theology polemically confronted, not accommodated, the surrounding cultural-religious systems of their day. Moreover, and to the point, regardless of how close a cultural value system is in exploring truth based on natural law (or, in the Jews' case, revealed law), they all fall short apart from the miracle of regeneration and the Spirit-led mind of Christ.

The Holy Spirit through Paul demonstrates that a major difference between unbelievers and believers is their mind-set: "For those who live according to the flesh set their minds on the things of the flesh, but those who live according to the Spirit set their minds on the things of the Spirit" (Romans 8:5). And the result of a person whose mind is set on the things of the Spirit is "life and peace" (Romans 8:6). What are those "things of the Spirit"? As referenced above, they are the "words not taught by human wisdom but taught by the Spirit, interpreting spiritual truths to those who are spiritual" (1 Corinthians 2:13).

The point is that the gospel is not a natural solution to a defined problem in every culture. Everyone knows they have a problem and are in trouble, but no one knows how to escape. Consequently, they try doing enough according to whatever code they have. But the truths of the gospel are spiritually discerned and are impossible to see as good news apart from the Spirit of God. People *cannot* and *will not* trust in Christ because it conflicts with their fallen nature. They are at enmity with God. "For the mind that is set on the flesh is hostile to God, for it does not submit to God's law; indeed, it cannot. Those who are in the flesh cannot please God" (Romans 8:7–8). They have neither the ability nor the desire apart from a miracle of the Spirit.

The "Gospel" of Three Cultural Value Systems

Some missiologists advocate nuancing the gospel (however they define it) based on the reality-interpreting lens and emphasis of a person's primary cultural value system. Many contemporary missionaries commonly assume one of three cultural value systems: fear/power, guilt/innocence, and shame/honor. I initially found these categories quite helpful to alert me to other value systems I do not easily discern, but after studying them and observing how missionaries indiscriminately latch onto new perspectives or effective strategies, I grew concerned with their theological imprecision. Moreover, I saw these contextualized explanations either confuse or mislead both indigenous believers and unbelievers alike.

The brief summaries below might sound terribly unsophisticated and underdeveloped. Yet, these are the typical explanations in missions trainings, discussions, seminars, and presentations by average practitioners:

- *Fear/Power Values:* For a person who views life through a fear/power value system, some missionaries propose that the gospel means that since people fearfully suffer under the power of Satan, they cannot live in the spiritual authority and rulership for which the sovereign Ruler created them. So Jesus died a death and was raised to a supremely authoritative position to disarm all the powers of darkness to restore power back to God's people. Therefore, to receive such divine power, a person must submit to Jesus as Lord and renounce dark powers.

- *Shame/Honor Values:* God created people to be part of His collective family to honor them as His children, but we all dishonor God, bringing about the shame that orphans us from His loving family. Jesus died an inglorious death to remove our shame and restore our honor so that when we honor God by loyalty to Christ, God then receives us into His family to bear His honorable name.

- *Guilt/Innocence Values:* God loves people and plans a good life for them. Our sins stand in the way of the holy God and us, and we cannot do enough good works. So Jesus died on the cross to take away the penalty of our sins so that whoever will turn to Jesus as their personal Savior and seek forgiveness of sins will receive eternal life.

Do these "gospel" presentations sound simplistic? Probably. Are they completely wrong? No. Are they imprecise and inaccurate? Yes. Are they blatantly man-centered? Sadly. Are they common? Definitely. Do these gospel presentations have any unifying center, or are they cultural estimations of an indefinable theological reality that is ethereal, dynamic, relational, and contextually situated? Is the mawkish sincerity of the person's heart and not the infinite transcendence of the truth all that really matters in God's eyes? The way some missionary-practitioners describe these is that they seem to be more like the six proverbial blind men touching the same elephant, each uniquely describing it as they feel around. One grabs the ear, another rubs the trunk, a third touches the tail, and so on. They each approximate what they believe to be true and relevant based on his experience and perspective.

Oftentimes, the average missionary on the field who hears such paradigms will uncritically adopt them and assume these are the next "silver bullet" for gospel witness. These three paradigms, indeed, can be quite helpful in missions training and short-term work to create initial awareness for the unseen reality of diverse cultural value systems. Truly, these paradigms represent different macro-cultural value systems through which the gospel travels. However, such presentations contain manifest errors. They require reexamination and recalibration to the biblical gospel. Arguments for presenting the gospel according to the dominant cultural value systems of a target culture often appeal to the non-Western, Eastern origin of the Scriptures. As the assumption goes, because God intends the Bible to be relevant to people of every tribe, tongue, and nation, there is meaning and interpretation in the Bible that might be discoverable from the standpoint of various socioeconomic experiences and diverse cultural value systems.

Guilt, Substitution, and Imputed Righteousness

Where the biblical gospel penetrates any cultural value system, at the center of the good news is *substitution*. For example, in a cultural value system of shame/honor, Jesus substitutes our shame for His honor. This substitutionary system similarly functions at the center of every other value system that reflects biblical categories. But what makes Christ able to substitute His earned benefits for our earned debt? Penal substitutionary atonement. Since our fundamental problem is that we are objectively guilty in Adam as our representative head, our penalty demands full satisfaction. Nevertheless, people in some cultural value systems might recognize their humanity is broken because of experiences of horizontal shame among their community or demonic fear in their religious rituals. But more significant and central to the brokenness of the horizontal human dilemma is the vertical objective guilt that demands satisfaction.

How are the benefits of Christ's substitutionary work made possible for His people? Through the act of *imputation*. Some will object that imputation is a Greco-Roman legal construct and medieval category forced upon the text that the Protestant Reformers blindly overapplied and, in the opinion of some, misapplied. They will also argue that it is not a word mentioned in the Bible. Such claims are deeply flawed, revealing a revisionist reading of church history and a myopic understanding of the Hebrew Scriptures, emerging more from trendy new perspectives on Paul than from church history or the Old and New Testaments.

Guilt/Righteousness Paradigm

We see that the Scriptural doctrines of substitution and imputation function as the linchpin for the "great exchange"—Christ's benefits for our debt, Christ's righteousness for our guilt, Christ's honor for our shame, Christ's peace for our fear, Christ's freedom for our bondage, Christ's strength for our weakness, and every other benefit and blessing He credits to us in exchange for our earned and deserved penalty. As we will see in the proceeding chapters, this great exchange is critical for understanding how believers in Christ receive through faith the benefits and blessings of cultural value systems (e.g., honor, peace, freedom, and strength) as they correspond to the gospel blessings found in Christ alone.

Missiologists and missionaries have commonly viewed innocence as the antithesis of guilt-oriented cultural value systems, just as shame is the antithesis of an honor-oriented value system. So, as the reasoning goes, we are guilty, and through the forgiveness of sins, we are innocent, or not guilty. But this model is fundamentally incomplete. Guilt and innocence are only corollaries in a modern nation-state that mandates not breaking the law (negatively) but does not require its perfect positive alternative. The state mandates no murder, but it does not mandate loving your neighbor as yourself. The state mandates

---

Guilt/Righteousness Value System Terms

Right. Wrong. Good. Bad. Wicked. Evil. Correct. True. False. Genuine. Hypocritical. Honest. Deceitful. Faithful. Unfaithful. Trustworthy. Deceptive. Law-Abiding. Duplicitous. Perfect. Upright. Blameless. Condemnation. Damnation. Sin. Innocent. Guiltless. Righteous. Iniquity. Credit. Impute. Reckon. Transgression. Trespass. Obedience. Disobedience. Lawful. Lawless. Forensic. Justice. Judicial. Just. Unjust. Judgment. Vindication. Justification. Acquittal. Rebellion. Virtuous. Depraved. Moral. Immoral. Ethical. Unethical. Court. Legal. Trial. Testimony. Charge. Fault. Accuse. Defense. Crime. Bondage. Prison. Rules. Code. Precept. Standard. Throne. Criminal. Boundary. Treaty. Ratify. Covenant. Punishment. Penalty. Debt. Atonement. Wrath. Pleasing. Displeasing. Due. Payment. Commendation. Recompense. Exact. Wrest. Acceptable. Approval. Remedy. Amend. Order. Test. Instruction. Commandment. Demand. Edict. Verdict. Decree. Grant. Measurement. Error. Blameworthy. Mediator. Intercessor. Merit. Offense. Fault. Forgiveness. Contrition. Breach. Fair. Violation. Requirement. Tenet. Regulation. Canon. Impartial. Unbiased. Equitable. Dereliction. Reprobate.

no rape, but it does not require directing your sexual desires only toward your spouse. But God does. More than innocence, God requires righteousness. And above state surveillance, God knows every thought and intent of the heart.

This guilt/innocence paradigm might work in contemporary law courts, but biblically and theologically, the antithesis of guilt is not merely guiltlessness. This is only half of the good news. The simplistic evangelical axiom that defines justification as "just as if I'd never sinned" is unexpectedly inaccurate. Rather, more precisely and in equally simple terms, justification is "just as if I were always righteous." The former highlights only what we did not do (never sin), while the latter highlights what we did do (always obey). Forgiveness indeed relates to the expiation of our guilt, leaving us amazingly innocent, and that is no small gift. Yet if we stop there, we must then conclude that in another cultural value system, like shame/honor, the equivalent would be to have our shame taken away, leaving us amazingly shameless. Again, no small gift. But for a shame/honor value system, similarly, that is only half the good news.

The point? Just as in a biblically defined shame/honor system where the full good news is that previously shameful people are now imputed with honor and thus treated as truly honorable, so in the guilt/righteousness value system, previously guilty people are now imputed with righteousness and thus treated as truly righteous. Forgiveness brings us to a neutral, innocent standing before God, whereas justification and the imputation of Christ's righteousness bring us to a righteous standing before God. God is against us no longer (being innocent), and moreover, He is truly, infinitely, immutably for us (being righteous). In a shame/honor system as understood biblically, God not only says to His child, "You are no longer shameful to Me," but He additionally says, "You are truly honorable to Me." Likewise, in a guilt/righteous-ness system, God not only says to His child, "You are no longer guilty before Me," but He says, "You are truly pleasing to Me." That is gloriously good news. That is why we must go beyond the guilt/innocence value system and contend for a guilt/righteousness system.

Trust Alone and Assurance

Because of how the term *faith* is so commonly used (e.g., the "Islamic faith," "faith journey," "interfaith dialogue," "my faith got me through," etc.), missiologists and theologians must define terms and deny assumptions. Using the word *trust*, generally, instead of *faith* seems preferable because trust gets at the heart of faith's theological import.

What should Christians mean by *faith*? Faith requires knowledge (*notitia*) of the truth and assent (*assensus*) to its veracity, yet even the demons know and acknowledge the truth (James 2:19). Faith is not less but more. It is resting, leaning, trusting (*fiducia*) in the truth. I must know gospel truth, agree that it is true, and trust that it is true for *me*. Faith is the instrument, not the ground, for our justification. God justifies by grace, through faith, in Christ.

Sects like the Word of Faith movement teach "faith in faith," but the Bible commends faith in Christ. The question, then, is not "*Did* you trust in Christ as your Savior?" which implies trusting in a point-in-time event or experience (i.e., your prayer to receive Christ). It is better to ask, "*Do* you trust in Christ as your Savior?" which implies trusting in Christ and is an improvement of the previous question. Even still, that yes/no question can suggest trusting in one's trust in Christ—finding assurance in the sense that one is *really* trusting in Him enough. Yet, to get to the heart of faith, we should ask an open-ended question: "Who is Christ, and what has He done for you?" Our answer to that question will reveal the object of our knowledge, assent, and hearty trust. Biblical faith is trust alone in *Christ*, not itself, not a feeling, not a memory, not right behavior, not a prayer, not a sacrament, not an experience.

Trust *alone* silences all self-assured boasting because it is devoid of all effort. Trust alone is not synonymous with trustworthiness, just as faith alone is not equal to faithfulness. No one trusts in their ability to lie on a hospital bed as a skilled surgeon removes a brain tumor. The trustworthiness of the surgeon to operate successfully is the object of the patient's trust. A parallel analogy more common to our daily experience is that of resting in a chair. No one trusts in their ability to hold themselves up as they relax in a chair. The sufficiency of the chair and its strength to hold the person's weight is the trustworthy feature. The person simply transfers their total weight to the chair, trusting alone in the chair's reliability to hold up. Either a person is fully sitting in a chair, resting in its strength, or awkwardly balancing, trying to squat and not fall. True resting trust is trust alone in the object of trust. The human experience understands this intuitively. No one lies awake at night, convincing themselves they are trusting enough in their mattress to keep them off the floor. They just rest on the mattress.

On board a commercial jet, when children ask their parents how they know the plane won't crash, the parent does not say, "Because I just believe," but assures them, "Because this is a trustworthy aircraft with a trustworthy pilot," which communicates knowledge, assent, and a hearty trust. Furthermore, the parent might indeed take comfort in their previous experiences: "I've endured bad turbulence before, and each time the pilot has landed the plane successfully. The crew has assured me that we are safe as long we stay buckled up and don't open the emergency door." Their devotion to stay seated and not open the door is merely indicative of their hearty trust and illustrative of their desire to honor the authority of the pilot, crew, and aircraft rules.

Who would risk taking their family into the sky on an uncertified, unreliable, derelict aircraft with an incompetent pilot? Moreover, no one assures themselves that their devotion to the pilot or the airline company will guarantee their arrival at their destination. Absurd and silly, that is contrary to natural experience and the normal use of language.

Our grasp of *faith* is essential for understanding how we access the benefits and blessings secured for us by Christ. And as we will see, it is critical for helping Christians coming out of works-oriented, karmic, reciprocity-based religions to rest in Christ's work and His promises for them. Instead of focusing on how strong our trust is (however we might subjectively measure it according to our feeling in the moment), we should rather look to Christ and the objective truth of the grace of God in uniting us to Him freely, fully, and forever. And trust *alone*, not in addition to anything, receives Christ and His righteousness by grace alone. Trust alone takes refuge in Christ Himself and His vicarious obedience and atonement, receiving Him and His benefits because He is benevolent and trustworthy and whom God has vindicated through the resurrection. Trust alone is at the center of the guilt/righteousness value system. From that center emerge the other biblical value systems and the free blessings of Christ's vicarious obedience—honor, peace, freedom, and strength.

Solutions through "Enoughness"

Most people in various cultures are not self-aware enough to tell you their cultural value system. Rarely will you hear someone say, "I don't think in terms of fear/peace; rather, I view life through a shame/honor lens." These are merely missiological tools we use to categorize ideas and determine our communication approaches.

Everyone knows something is wrong with themselves and the world. Philosophers, therapists, politicians, and religious leaders all create systems that approximate the good, true, and beautiful based on "human wisdom" (1 Corinthians 2:13). But all human systems of interpreting reality, locating the problem to which their conscience is pointing, and proposing a solution are futile and under the domination of the curse and the spirit of the age.

As the Puritan preacher John Bunyan (1628–1688) wrote in his famous *The Pilgrim's Progress*, Christian's burden dominated his consciousness. Before losing his burden at the cross, Christian heeded the advice of Mr. Worldly Wiseman from the town called Carnal Policy. Worldly Wiseman counseled him to go to the village called Morality and seek out the help of Legalism or Civility. And to get there, he must first follow the path up the mountain. The mountain represents Sinai, indicating that worldly wisdom always requires law. Christian's burden would supposedly diminish only when he had followed the advice of Legalism and Civility enough. He would then enjoy the benefits and blessings of no more conviction of sin. Likewise, every cultural value system has a Worldly Wiseman, as it were, who guarantees blessing and benefits through enough rules, practices, instructions, codes, rituals, and laws. In the end, all paths lead to Sinai. And Sinai only supplies a heavy burden.

Every culture is complex and an amalgamation of overlapping cultural value systems. Moreover, every individual is even more multifaceted and a recipient of multiple cultural value systems influenced by family, media, language, socioeconomic status, religion, personality, experiences, and the like. How do we locate the original problem their system is seeking to solve? A way for discovering their fallen solution to their fallen perception of their problem is to observe what they are trying to do enough of in order to assuage their conscience. In other words, what is it they do—if they could only do it enough—that would finally remove their burden and award them honor, peace, freedom, or power? We are essentially looking for traces and evidence of their own system of self-justification.

One way to detect the enoughness of each value system and individual is, positively speaking, to look at the habits, rituals, desires, and goals they are seeking to merit. If they could only please their father enough, pray toward Mecca enough, spin the prayer wheels enough, recite their mantras enough, appease the ancestral spirits enough, and liberate their inner selves enough, then they would secure their felt needs of peace, honor, freedom, or strength.

Conversely, another way to determine the enoughness of a value system or an individual is, negatively speaking, to consider what they are seeking to avoid through doing enough: doing enough to avoid bringing shame upon their family name, praying enough to escape the fear of demonic retribution, living sacrificially enough to avoid selfishness, campaigning enough for the right political revolution to achieve upward mobility, or giving enough to the miracle worker or shaman to be rid of weakness and infirmity. These all reveal that everyone knows there is a problem and that everyone knows the perceived solution requires enough merits.

Deep down inside, everyone honestly knows they can never do enough. They need a substitute. Some might be so spiritually blind and self-deceived that they think they can do enough. But on their death bed, if they're coherent, they know it was never enough, and now it's too late. Human wisdom and fallen cultural value systems are all insufficient. As the Bible says, "They have no knowledge, who carry around their wooden idol and pray to a god who cannot save. . . . And there is no other God besides Me, a righteous God and a Savior; there is none except Me. 'Turn to Me and be saved, all the ends of the earth'" (Isaiah 45:20–22 NASB95). The truth that Christ is enough as our Righteous One and Substitute, who will exchange His righteousness and blessings for our guilt and curse, is spiritually discerned.

Practical Applications

Pre-Evangelism Preparation:
Questions to Ask Your Target Culture

1. What do they believe is the problem for all people?

2. What are their cultural virtues and vices?

3. What are their rituals? Habits?

4. If they did not do their rituals and obey the controlling code of their consciences enough, what do they think would be the outcome?

5. Ask questions of authority and source: Why do they think that? Who told them that? How do they know this?

6. Pre-Evangelism Reflection: Questions to Ask Yourself

7. Have I unnecessarily validated their perceived problem and corresponding solution?

8. Have I asked questions that help them question the authority and source of their problem/solution system?

9. What have I discovered to be their rituals of "enoughness," and what does that tell me about the problem for which they are seeking a solution?

10. Have I helped them consider when they have done enough? How do they know? Who or what is their source and authority? How do they define their terms? What do they mean? Are they sure?

11. When and how can I show them the futility of self-justification? How might this lead to their repentance?

12. When and to what extent can I explain the biblical doctrine of original sin, Christ's righteousness, His substitutionary atonement, and the great exchange through faith alone?

13. What other core doctrines should I be prepared to teach them? How can I make sure they understand what I mean and don't mean when I talk about God, creation, man, sin, Christ, and faith/repentance?

Discipleship Applications

Christians all over the world, though blessed with the mind of Christ, still struggle with the old ways of meriting blessing. This is part of fallen human nature; we all do it. This challenge for discipleship is really an opportunity for great joy in Christ. When we first evaluate our own anesthetizing behaviors (those things we do to numb our disappointment with our ongoing battle with sin) and meritorious efforts (those things we do enough to ensure God's ongoing blessing in our life), and when we can instead learn to heartily rest in God's eternal, immutable, infinite grace in Christ, then we can help other Christians be free of their attempts at maintaining God's favor through enoughness. The major fault line underneath our Christianized versions of trusting in enoughness (surrendering enough, singing passionately enough, praying long enough, donating enough, busy at church enough, avoiding worldly influences enough) is that it fails to understand grace alone and faith alone.

The battle for Christian growth and discipleship is to know, assent, and trust alone in Christ's work in our place on our behalf from beginning to end. We don't get saved by faith and then stay saved by doing enough. He is the Author and Perfector of our faith, and from start to finish, this is a grace race. Christians will learn to receive and rest in the benefits and blessings of Christ's honor, peace, freedom, and strength as they rest assured in His decisive exchange on the cross—our guilt for His righteousness. Christ's substitutionary atonement and earned righteousness for us are the immutable ground for enjoying infinite and eternal honor, peace, freedom, and strength.

Bringing It to Center

People and cultures are multidimensional in that they comprise several overlapping value systems and orientations. For instance, in one Muslim country in which I served, my friends would tell me they live like immoral Europeans but think like fundamentalist Arabs, though they spoke neither Arabic nor a European language. I soon realized how interesting and yet similar we all are. Despite all the ethnolinguistic, cultural, and existential complexities, one thing about all humans is the same: we are all guilty in Adam, and no one does good, not even one. Each of us needs an external righteousness and a Substitute. Seeking to escape the curse and achieve the blessings and benefits of righteousness, all people try to do enough. But in all our deepest sincerity and best efforts, our enough is never enough. But there is a Righteous One whose righteousness is enough for all who turn from the futility of their own enoughness and trust in Him alone. His penal substitutionary atonement on our behalf is enough to expiate our guilt. By grace alone through trust alone in Him alone, we can be declared righteous and enjoy all the blessings and benefits of honor, peace, freedom, and strength. And all this is for the praise of the glory of His grace.

They lift up their voices, they sing for joy;
over the majesty of the LORD they shout from the west.
Therefore in the east give glory to the LORD;
in the coastlands of the sea, give glory to the name of the
LORD, the God of Israel.
From the ends of the earth we hear songs of praise,
of glory to the Righteous One.
– Isaiah 24:14–16

CHAPTER 3

Christ
Our Honor

Have you ever visited a rice farm? Maybe you've seen picturesque photographs of lush rice fields terraced on a hillside in a remote jungle setting. Such pictures are indeed quite lovely, but something that is sometimes missing from them is all the families who normally work those fields. Rice farmers are classic collectivists: families find strength and security in working together, equally sharing in the labor and in the harvest. Their millennia-long codes of shame/honor ensure order, equity, and fidelity are for the common good. Their sense of right and wrong, good and evil, is bound up in their language of caring for one another. For example, it would be pure evil to forsake and abandon a family member, and the gravity of such evil would take on the shame/honor language of *betrayal*, which in some collectivistic cultures is the greatest evil. In cultural

> **Shame/Honor Value System Terms**
>
> Face. Humiliation. Status. Reputation. Glory. Scorn. Abandonment. Ridicule. Approval. Disapproval. Fame. Renown. Reproach. Belonging. Betrayal. Praise. Loyalty. Family name. Defilement. Desecration. Veneration.

orientations that appear to be communal or familial, we typically call them collectivistic. But since no single static collectivistic culture exists, we use the word *orientation* to describe their tendencies.

The dominant cultural value systems of these orientations are typically shame/honor. In missions studies, it is popular to address the gospel in shame/honor systems in terms of Christ as King and faith as allegiance. People in shame/honor cultures might easily conceptualize terms like *king, emperor, ruler, monarch, lord,* and *sovereign,* but their understanding of those titles and the Bible's description of Christ as Lord are not alike. In elevating the lordship of Jesus, we must take the truth up past the level of kingship, all the way up to the name that LORD indicates—Yahweh. The New Testament calls Jesus *kurios* (Lord), which is the Greek translation for Yahweh in the Septuagint. Jesus is the *christos* (Christ), which is the Greek translation for Messiah-King or Anointed One in the Septuagint—the anointed Son of David.[3]

The Gospel for Shame/Honor Value Systems

When Christians say, "Jesus Christ is Lord," they are saying, "King Jesus is Yahweh." This gives Christ's kingship a more salvific shade of meaning and more theological cohesion to Yahweh's self-revelation throughout the Scriptures. He is Israel's God who uses His sovereign power and authority to save sinners. Jesus is not mainly king as the nations might understand a monarch. Rather, He is God's Anointed One on whom God has bestowed the name of Yahweh—the image and face of Israel's covenant-keeping Deliverer-God.

To be clear about what God expects for inheriting eternal life, Jesus summed up the law as loving God with sincere,

---

3   Jesus Messiah is identified as Son of God and Son of David—the divine King. For example, see John 1:43–51.

wholehearted fidelity and loving one's neighbor as oneself. A man asked Jesus, "'Teacher, what shall I do to inherit eternal life?' He said to him, 'What is written in the Law? How do you read it?' And he answered, 'You shall love the Lord your God with all your heart and with all your soul and with all your strength and with all your mind, and your neighbor as yourself.' And he said to him, 'You have answered correctly; do this, and you will live'" (Luke 10:25–28). But is this possible? Even if we could perfectly love God in complete honoring allegiance to Him for a moment, could we ever do it enough? Always? Did Christ die to merely make us savable? Is the good news that Christ made an opportunity possible for us to receive eternal life if we have enough loyal allegiance? If inheriting eternal life through enough loyal faithfulness to God were possible, "then Christ died for no purpose" (Galatians 2:21).

In the biblical narrative, God fulfilled His unilateral promise to Abraham by graciously giving the land to Israel (Galatians 3:16; 4:24–26), fulfilling the promise of "seeds" (plural), descendants as numerous as the stars and sand. God gave them the temporal land through Joshua's leadership. But this is different from the second promise to Abraham's "Seed" (singular), which Scripture clarifies is Christ, in whom God's eternal promises finally find their *telos* (Galatians 3:16–18). The subsequent giving of the Mosaic law, hundreds of years later, never annulled God's promise to bless the nations with the Spirit through Abraham's Seed (Galatians 3:14, 17–18). The law merely demonstrated the utter hopelessness and despair of trying to please God enough through loyal faithfulness to Him, pointing transgressors (lawbreakers) to justification through trust (not trustworthiness) in Christ (Galatians 3:21–24). The Bible clearly states:

> All who rely on works of the law are under a curse; for it is written, "Cursed be everyone who does not abide by all things written in the Book of the Law, and do them."

> Now it is evident that no one is justified before God by the law, for "The righteous shall live by faith." But the law is not of faith, rather "The one who does them shall live by them." Christ redeemed us from the curse of the law by becoming a curse for us—for it is written, "Cursed is everyone who is hanged on a tree"—so that in Christ Jesus the blessing of Abraham might come to the Gentiles, so that we might receive the promised Spirit through faith. (Galatians 3:10–14)

Notice, it does not say, "Cursed be everyone who does not try hard enough, surrender all, follow with abandoned devotion, sincerely mean well, or make every effort with good intentions." Nor does it say, "The one who strives earnestly or serves as faithfully as possible."

Faith Alone for Shame/Honor

Faith/trust cannot equal faithfulness/trustworthiness. *Faith* is starkly contrasted with "works of the law"—faithfulness in loving God and neighbor (Deuteronomy 6:5; Leviticus 19:18; Galatians 5:1–6, 14). The Holy Spirit through Paul confronts anyone who thinks they can be good enough for God. Paul lists his unrivaled sevenfold pedigree for law-keeping of ethnic purity, heartfelt zeal, purity of doctrine, and blameless loyalty to God's law (Philippians 3:4–6), which still failed the "enoughness" test. Paul rested in the truth that he was found in Christ, not that he was pleasing enough to God through his best attempt at faithfulness but through having a righteousness "which comes through faith in Christ, the righteousness from God that depends on faith" (Philippians 3:9).

When a gospel message mainly emphasizes the blessings of what we should do in this life (faithfully surrendering to the kingship of Christ) or the blessings of what we can get in this life (faithfully following in the ways of Jesus to experience abundant life), such good news doesn't compute with those who languish under the tyranny of a terminal diagnosis, chronic pain, chronic fatigue, devastating depression, secret abuse, and totalitarian oppression. When a sinner is slipping away on their deathbed, they want to know where to find forgiveness and atonement. Their time has expired. Their life is behind them. Death is at the door. Don't tell them that the good news is that Jesus is King and that they must only be loyal to Him or that Jesus can give them purpose if they just walk faithfully in imitation of Christ. Their dilemma, then, is "Faithful, how much? Faithful, how long? When is enough, enough?" That's not good news. The good news is that Jesus is the King of Glory who uses His divine authority and power to save guilty sinners who rest and take refuge in Him alone. He is the sovereign Savior. Such *sola fide* honors Him for who He is—the King who saves sinners. He is our glorious King because He is our good Savior. The truth is that *sola fide* focuses on Christ alone as the object of its trust, whereas allegiance and faithfulness might claim to focus on Christ, but in practice, they focus on "doing" and "enoughness"—loyal enough, surrendered enough, submitted enough, faithful enough.

Such temporally focused explanations of following Christ or being loyal to Christ might indeed connect with the cultural orientation and appeal to the sentiments of Buddhists, Muslims, Hindus, and anyone else leaving a merits-based religious system. The conceptual hurdles to Christianity would be lessened. No doubt, this is a reason why focusing on faithfulness and loyalty to God is popular among missionaries who want to share the gospel in shame/honor paradigms. Yet, whether expressed or not, the troubled heart in us all wonders, "Since my love for God and neighbor is never perfect and always in need of improvement, what then? How does God measure my faithfulness and determine it's enough?"

The problem is that many easily confuse justification and sanctification categories and verses. We truly walk in *sanctified* faithfulness, but our faithfulness is not *sanctifying*. Because of Christ's sanctifying obedience on our behalf, God rewards our obedience by grace (not merit) as sanctified faithfulness. The faithfulness we trust to save us from hell on the last day is the faithfulness we trust to initially justify us. It is the same faithfulness. We are indeed saved by faithfulness, but not our own— Christ's faithfulness alone imputed to us, received through trust alone, from start to finish.

My hope is that many missionaries who speak of salvation through loyally honoring God would agree with these statements. I hope they even seek to improve their language so as to not mislead young believers who are former merit-seekers through inadvertently promoting a gospel that sounds like another merit-oriented religion. Yet, others, when pressed on these issues, will become defensive and argue that the classic Protestant doctrine of justification by grace alone through faith alone is an artifact of a bygone era, answering theological questions few ask anymore. At best, they are making a grave error of confusing or prioritizing sanctification verses/categories over justification verses/categories.

Calling people to be "followers of Christ" is a good thing and has gained popularity over against calling people to "receive Christ," which to some implies mere intellectual assent and easy-believism. Though the two are important and biblical, they are not synonymous. Following Christ is a call to discipleship (as a rabbi would select and instruct his students) that presupposes regeneration, but it can easily devolve into law-preaching if we don't intentionally ground it in the grace of the gospel. But Christ's call to discipleship can wound the consciences of guilty sinners to push them to escape to Him for righteousness. Receiving Christ is a call to rest and trust in Him with saving faith. The two calls must not become rivals, yet we must carefully distinguish them. The free, gracious offer of the good news is to and for shameful, weak, fearful, shackled, guilty sinners. Then, after He has graciously bestowed new birth and true, hearty faith, Jesus calls them to follow Him as disciples.

Guilt/Righteousness for Shame/Honor

Throughout the Bible, many narratives and didactic teachings confirm a shame/honor value system. As previously mentioned, the way the Bible teaches shame/honor paradigms differs from fallen cultural approximations of similar paradigms. Similarly, though shame/honor is assumed beneath the collectivistic cultural orientation, collectivism, as commonly understood in the world, is not a biblical concept.

Loving God and others is no collective campaign, though it is indeed a community effort. We each are responsible for being faithful to God, and when we fail, we each are responsible, individually, to trust in Christ for salvation. We are guilty by solidarity with Adam, and we are righteous by solidarity with Christ. Under those two representative heads, we stand as individuals before God. The Bible never kowtows to fallen cultural expressions of the spirit of the age, regardless of how they might approximate the good, true, and beautiful of the inherent image of God in mankind.

The Bible clearly teaches that at the heart of biblical shame is objective guilt. The emotions of shame in Genesis 3:10 follow in the wake of the guilt of Genesis 3:6. Throughout Scripture, the emotional and communal shame of sexual perversion, for instance, is commensurate to its objective guilt (e.g., Leviticus 20:17–19). Shame is derivative of guilt, just as expiation is derivative of propitiation. Penal substitutionary atonement is the solution to the guilt problem, and insofar as God propitiates His wrath on the cross due our guilt, He expiates our guilt and thus removes our shame. If Jesus only went outside Jerusalem carrying a cross never to be seen again, like a scapegoat departing the camp for the wilderness, this would neither satisfy God's justice nor would it secure the benefits of His redeeming work. The center of Christ's work was penal substitutionary atonement because the center of our problem was Adamic guilt. And from that center emanates the solution to our shame problem.[4]

The Great Exchange

Though worldly cultures typically treat shame as a horizontal problem, the Bible overwhelmingly treats shame as a vertical problem—an example of how biblical categories confront and reorder worldly categories. That is not to say that the Bible speaks nothing of horizontal shame in community. It does indeed. But the biblical data's proportionality prioritizes vertical shame. The problem with all sinners is that though they are aware of their shame before one another, they have suppressed the moral law on their hearts that tells them they are guilty of offending a holy God, which in itself will bring them immeasurable, eternal shame. Evil leads to defilement and dishonor. The problem with evil is that it needs judgment. It needs a Substitute. Honor to God can only be secured by Christ's faithfulness to Him.

Through faith, we receive Christ's honoring obedience and wrath-bearing atonement to God for us. It's the double imputation of honor and shame: Christ's God-honoring life imputed to us through faith alone, and our God-shaming life imputed to Christ on the cross—the shame of our curse and guilt exchanged for the honor of Christ's blessing and righteousness. And it is all received fully, freely, and forever through trust alone in Christ alone. The God-honoring life we now live is the Spirit-filled life of faith alone in the pleasing Son of God.

---

4   Consider a few examples of this pattern in the Bible: Ezra 9:6–7; Isaiah 6:5–7; Daniel 9:7–15.

Counterfeit Honor

The world is full of people who are self-assured that they are honorable enough. They believe they are faithful and loyal enough. Yet, their heart's internal moral code nags and torments them that they are never helpful enough to their parents, generous enough to the poor, respectful enough to their authorities, routine enough in religious rituals, and shrewd enough to get away with secret, shameful acts. So, they scheme ways to bribe, deceive, cheat, and steal, all for the sake of maintaining the public impression that they are respectable and worthy of renowned reputation. In a sense, their gospel is self-justification by achieving enough honor. This is simply the corrupt heart's way within a given cultural value system of seeking to placate surfaced knowledge of sin. Their conscience feels convicted because of Adamic guilt and personal transgression of the law of God on their heart.

Practical Applications

A Pre-Evangelism Conversation

Abdul was an Iraqi student with whom I played soccer/football and had many conversations about religion, history, the Qur'an, and Christianity[5]

> Missionary: "In your opinion, if you could change one thing in the world for the better, what would it be?"

> Abdul: "I am different than you Westerners because I don't try to have my own opinions. I try to uphold what my family has believed. We are Muslims, and we try to keep *Shariah* law. We follow the 'Five Pillars.'"

---

5 For a corresponding conversation with Abdul, see chapter 6 in Burns, Ancient Gospel, Brave New World.

M: "Okay, you're right; my question was too individualistic and self-oriented. Tell me about your family and what you believe."

A: "In my family, we look out for one another. We are loyal, and we want to be good Muslims. My father is a good man, and I'm working hard to help him as he gets older."

M: "That's very honorable of you. It takes a lot of virtue to care about someone else so much. What is it that motivates your devotion? When would you feel like you have done enough for him?"

A: "First, we believe it's the right thing to do—to honor our parents. Second, we know we must do good to get to Paradise, and what is better than honoring our parents? And to answer your other question, I don't know when I've done enough. I suppose, maybe when he's really happy with me."

M: "Have you always loved your father and honored him above yourself? What do you think Allah would say?"

A: "I don't know. I just know that if I do right enough, I'll make it."

M: "Make it where? What's the alternative?"

A: "I'll get to Paradise. But if I am not a good enough son and Muslim, I'll suffer eternal punishment."

M: "How do you know this? Who told you? Why do you believe it?"

A Simple Gospel Explanation

The following brief explanation would come after multiple occasions of pre-evangelism questions and even more opportunities of laying a framework for the biblical storyline and its core doctrines of revelation, God, creation, man, sin, and Christ:

> The Bible teaches that God is the most honorable being in existence. God defines all of existence, and He determines what is truly honorable and shameful. Those gut-wrenching feelings of shame that we experience in this life—humiliating our family, disgracing our teacher, betraying our country—are echoes of eternal shame we will suffer under the wrath of God forever. But those shameful feelings point to a bigger problem. The ultimate problem is that our original forefather, Adam, turned his back on his Creator by doing what was right in his own eyes. In devotion to His holy name, God condemned Adam and his progeny as guilty. As part of Adam's family, we break God's law by nature. We are born rebels and enemies of God. Yet, God in His mercy with which He loved us before He even created the world, chose us to be part of His family and share in His family honor. So, He sent His Son, Jesus, to live a life of loving Him and loving others perfectly—the law-keeping life we should have lived but could not and would not. And then Jesus, after perfectly pleasing God and His law, did the most obedient act: He died on an inglorious Roman cross, and God was honored to punish Him for our shameful guilt. He took away the curse of our shame. So, by no sincere effort of our own but only through resting in Christ alone and turning from trying to do enough to achieve honor can we be declared righteous with His righteousness. Then the Father legally adopts us into His family, and we partake in the blessings of Christ's reputation and name. God's Spirit testifies (like a defense attorney) to our spirit that we are heirs of God, fellow heirs with Christ. God did this so that we would glorify Him for His grace and enjoy Him forever.

Discipleship Applications

Those new Christians who come from shame/honor cultural value systems typically experience two dominant motivators for Christian growth: desire to honor God to maintain God's favor or desire to honor God to make up for a shameful past. This is not the case for every Christian, but it's quite common, nonetheless.

First, let us remind one another that not all shame experienced in the Christian life is worthy of repentance and despair. Shame suffered because of persecution for Christ's sake is indeed an honor worthy of rejoicing: "Blessed are you when others revile you and persecute you and utter all kinds of evil against you falsely on my account. Rejoice and be glad, for your reward is great in heaven" (Matthew 5:11–12), and "if anyone suffers as a Christian, let him not be ashamed, but let him glorify God in that name" (1 Peter 4:16).

Second, there is a shame that propels our pursuit of holiness: "Become sober-minded as you ought, and stop sinning; for some have no knowledge of God. I speak this to your shame" (1 Corinthians 15:34 NASB95).[6] A true fear of God should stir in us an aversion to that which is shameful to God and an affection for that which is honoring to Him. It's because we love Him so much and revere His good and awesome name.

Third and most commonly, poor, beleaguered souls march through the Christian life with a stiff upper lip out of dutiful servitude to an honor-demanding God, seeking to pay Him back for His benevolent patronage. Deep inside, we all know we can never pay God back, but an unsanctified shame/honor paradigm might lead a young Christian to believe they at least must try, hoping that somehow God will see their sincere effort and deem

---

6   See also 1 Corinthians 6:5; Romans 6:21; 2 Thessalonians 3:14.

them honorable enough. But our allegiance to God is never loyal
or honorable enough. Never. This is terrifyingly bad news for
those who come from merits-based religious systems of reciproc-
ity. They are like a bruised reed and a smoldering wick, and we
must tenderly guide them to Jesus, who will neither break them
nor smolder them (Isaiah 42:3; Matthew 12:20). Here are some
sweet promises to assuage the ashamed, troubled soul:

- Whoever believes in him will not be put to shame. (Romans
  9:33; see also 10:11)

- But with you there is forgiveness, that you may be feared.
  (Psalm 130:4)

- The friendship of the LORD is for those who fear him, and he
  makes known to them his covenant. (Psalm 25:14)

- Seek the LORD while he may be found; call upon him while
  he is near; let the wicked forsake his way, and the unrighteous man his thoughts; let him return to the LORD, that he
  may have compassion on him, and to our God, for he will
  abundantly pardon. (Isaiah 55:6–7)

- All that the Father gives me will come to me, and whoever
  comes to me I will never cast out. (John 6:37)

- If we confess our sins, he is faithful and just to forgive us our
  sins and to cleanse us from all unrighteousness. (1 John 1:9)

- Come to me, all who labor and are heavy laden, and I will
  give you rest. Take my yoke upon you, and learn from me,
  for I am gentle and lowly in heart, and you will find rest
  for your souls. For my yoke is easy, and my burden is light.
  (Matthew 11:28–30)

Bringing It to Center

The shame/honor cultural paradigm pervades most cultures in the world. Even in places like the West where individualism reigns, a strong aversion to shame and humiliation drives people. God is so good to save us from judgment and count us righteous in Christ and then to go on to secure for us all the blessings of honorable sonship to be enjoyed in His family, never to be rescinded or diminished. We can do nothing to improve on God's pleasure in us, nor can we do anything to break it. On all those who rest in Christ alone as their Substitute and Righteousness, God bestows immutable, infinite, and eternal honor. And in grateful, worshipful response, we seek to glorify Him for His sovereign grace.

> For with the heart a person believes, resulting in righteousness, and with the mouth he confesses, resulting in salvation. For the Scripture says, "Whoever believes in Him will not be put to shame." For there is no distinction between Jew and Greek; for the same Lord is Lord of all, abounding in riches for all who call on Him.
> – Romans 10:10–12 NASB95
> [7]

---

7   In the NASB 1995 edition it says, "Whoever believes in Him will not be disappointed," but the translation here in the 2020 edition for "disappointed" is better rendered as "put to shame."

CHAPTER 4

Christ
Our Peace

Think of stories you've heard about spiritualistic rituals. Maybe you've seen a movie or a documentary that portrays disturbing demonic activity. What do we commonly imagine when we think of animistic tribes in remote jungles or shamanistic healing rituals? When we think of spiritualism, we often think of Hollywood's version of demon possession, angelic manifestations, shamanistic rituals, and witch-doctor remedies. Demonic phenomena indeed occur, and I have witnessed some in various contexts around the world. Yet these animistic aspects are typically isolated varieties of a much larger spiritualistic orientation that encompasses many communities and cultures around the world.

The orientation and tendency toward spiritualism pervade the worldwide community, and its ranks are growing every year. Increasingly, people are exploring New Age, mystical, and Eastern spiritualities. Spiritualistic orientations can overlap various African, Native American, Caribbean, and other tribal animistic practices. No single, static spiritualistic orientation exists. However, upon surveying the spread of ideas through the internet pumped relentlessly into the hands of people in once isolated communities, change is afoot—a growing influence of malleable Buddhism-inspired New Ageism marketed through popular global culture. In fact, traditional Buddhist countries are beginning to adopt the trendy Westernized version of Buddhism. Increasingly, popular karma-related ideas, more than traditional animism, dominate cultures of spiritualistic orientation.

Spiritual Warfare and Truth

In cultures of spiritualistic orientation, multiple layers of fear/ peace, bondage/freedom, and weakness/strength exist on a continuum. One challenge of addressing the demonic is that often we misunderstand the devices of demons and consign their work predominantly to the perceptible, mystical, and experiential—physical ailments, menacing intuitions, vivid nightmares, ominous premonitions, territorial strongholds, paranormal sensations, inciting habitual sins, and the like. Typically, many presume that demons inflict harm and cause fear, so then people desire power to overcome such demon-induced fear. True, to be set free from demonic oppression we need a power greater than ourselves. However, power is essentially a *means* for peace, and that's what we all finally want. And in karmic cultures, the pervasiveness of fear is palpable.

Sometimes people are truly aware of the evil spirits around them, especially in the temples and sacred sites. But their conscious daily experience is not so fixated on the presence of the demons as it is on the *lies* of demons that haunt their thinking, temptations to sin, superstitions, and anxious decision-making. So it is, also, with karma-background Christians. They may indeed retain an intuition about the demonic based on their previous religious rituals, but the fear they suffer most is not so much from regular manifest encounters with evil spirits as much as from believing doctrines of demons that the gospel of peace has yet to vanquish.

The Holy Spirit through Paul says, "For the weapons of our warfare are not of the flesh but have divine power to destroy strongholds. We destroy arguments and every lofty opinion raised against the knowledge of God, and take every thought captive to obey Christ" (2 Corinthians 10:4–5). Therefore, since a Christian's assault on the enemy is through destroying arguments and lofty opinions raised against the knowledge of God, then, conversely, the enemy's main tactic is through arguments, speculations, opinions, and any other counterfeit claim that diminishes, obfuscates, and perverts the knowledge of God. Satan's strategy is essentially the same for both unbelievers and believers alike.

According to this passage, biblical spiritual warfare, then, prioritizes gospel encounters over against popular methods that typically emphasize deliverance, binding spirits, discerning demonic strongholds, spiritual mapping, healing prayer, and the like. Our spiritual weapons obliterate fortresses of lies raised up against God when the gospel of peace brings truth to oppressed, confused, deceived, and frightened souls.

The Gospel for Fear/ Peace Value Systems

In Scripture, numerous synonymous terms exist for the concept of peace. At a basic level, the Hebrew word *shalom* captures the idea well. It is the notion that all is well; God is pleased; nothing can ultimately harm you; God's favor rests on you fully, freely, and forever.

Fear/Peace Value System Terms

Merit. Duty. Righteousness. Burden. Obligation. Recompense. Karma. Fear. Afraid. Anxiety. Panic. Brokenness. Nervousness. Worry. Calamity. Confusion. Catastrophe. Ritual. Cataclysm. Curse. Tragedy. Shalom. Blessing. Comfort. Wholeness. Wellness. Protection. Stability. Peace. Danger. Threat. Assurance. Tranquility. Harmony. Contentment.

Sometimes Scripture uses the word *peace*, while sometimes it uses a synonymous idea, similarly with its opposing parallel—*fear*.

Moreover, *fear* and *peace* theologically and textually often overlap and complement shame/honor, weakness/strength, and bondage/freedom cultural value paradigms. *Fear* and *power*, though popularly used in missiological conversations, do not correspond conceptually or biblically. Fear is a subjective feeling rooted in a threat, and though power may mitigate the threat, power is not the ultimate subjective replacement of fear. Peace is. Power and strength are qualities of condition, like their common antitheses—weakness and vulnerability.

Fear-based service to God emerges from the unattainable demands of the law. The law requires complete, wholehearted obedience to everything written in it, creating fear. But the gospel declares that Christ has become the curse of the law and has fulfilled it for all who through faith are united to Him, establishing peace. The problem is when we confuse the fearfulness of the law's demands that should drive us to trust in Christ's work alone for our justification with the comfort of the gospel's declaration that should drive us to trust in Christ's work alone for our lifelong sanctification.

Many Christians in fear/peace cultural value systems devoutly practice "Christian" rituals and routines to maintain God's blessings and to avoid punishment through calamity. This is not much different from the karmic systems out of which they converted to Christianity. Desiring ongoing assurance of God's love and enjoyment of His peace pushes us on the merry-go-round of doing our best to love Him wholeheartedly and to love people as ourselves. Fear gains a foothold in our hearts if we offer anything less than our best. Our problem is that we live under the effects of the curse and realize that, deep down inside, our best is never enough—good enough, loving enough, honorable enough, strong enough, pure enough. Though people in all cultures feel fear, their perceptions of what is fearful often do not connect with what is truly fearful—God.

Our peace and confident standing before God are on the ground of sovereign, immutable, extravagant grace, which we received through trust alone in Christ's work alone for us. Unlike the seraphim who fly around the throne of God, covering their feet for fear of standing in His holy presence (Isaiah 6:2), we stand united to Christ in His righteous covering, honored and adored in the presence of our Father. The Christian should feel no fear of a fickle God, capricious like Allah or vengeful like mystical powers exacting karmic retribution on those whose best is never enough. Too often, karma-background believers fall back into the old ruts of routines and rituals in pursuit of "enoughness" to ensure blessing. But our minds should be at peace, knowing that the Spirit dwells within us, freeing us from the burden of the law on our hearts (Romans 8:4–6).

Faith Alone for Fear/Peace

To some, faith is what you need in order to get saved at conversion, and favor is what you need to access God's blessings and sometimes to stay saved altogether. For those believers who come from pervasively animistic backgrounds, a temptation exists to do good enough to secure God's peace and protection from evil spirits. In many fear/peace cultural value systems, signs of blessing and favor are rain, harvest, health, food, shelter, family stability, employment, no demonic nightmares, money in the bank, good looks, and sons. Christians from such superstitious and karmic backgrounds struggle with the idea of God's favor.

They love stories about success (like Joseph) and overcoming threats (like David and Goliath). They read about Noah, who followed God while the rest of the world drowned itself in its own decadence even before they physically drowned in the flood. And the key to being like Noah and walking in God's protection and blessing, as opposed to suffering His punitive judgment, is this: "But Noah found favor in the eyes of the Lord" (Genesis 6:8).

Depending on the language, *favor* often implies *favorite*, which requires doing something extraordinary (above and beyond ordinary) to merit preferred status of an authority or patron. But this word for *favor* is the Hebrew word for *grace*, which doctrinally means "electing grace"—God's eternal, sovereign choice to bestow grace on sinners and save them for Himself, apart from anything they could merit.

Through faith alone in God and His promises, we receive Christ and all that He is for us. Because of God's electing favor, we are eternally united to Christ based on His righteousness credited to us. We have no need to fear because God has forensically secured and filially adopted us. Our subjective peace with God rests on our objective peace with God. The blessings that flow through faith in that righteous union supply life and peace.

Guilt/Righteousness for Fear/Peace

Though some think power is the antidote to fear, since the perceived desire in some cultures is to access power (mantras, shamanism, crystals, amulets, etc.) to dispel fear, the truly biblical solution to the fear problem is peace—peace from God and peace with God. He wields His sovereign power to bring about peace, namely in the resurrection of the Righteous One for our justification. His power is the pathway out of our fear into His peace. And God indelibly anchors our peace to the removal of our guilt, our union with Christ, and the imputation of Christ's sufficient, God-pleasing righteousness.

The challenge is to translate our horizontal fears and calibrate them in light of true vertical fear. Genuine biblical peace issues from genuine biblical fear of God—not punitive fear but filial fear. Fearing God as our holy Father produces peace-filled living, knowing that God is for us and never against us. Fearing God as our holy Judge, knowing that we are doubly guilty—condemned in Adam and awaiting trial for our own transgressions—should cause us to escape to Christ. For we find refuge in His substitutionary atonement and free righteousness, obtaining access to reconciliation with God and a divine peace as infinite, eternal, and immutable as God Himself.

The Bible teaches that at the heart of biblical peace is first fear emerging out of objective guilt—a guilt that demands eternal death. Guilt is the ground of true fear, and so union with Christ in His substitutionary death and resurrection and the imputation of righteousness in justification is the ground of true peace.[8]

The Great Exchange

Knowing that His followers would be tempted to fear what the world fears—and what the world fears most commonly is violence inflicted upon the helpless—Jesus said, "Do not fear those who kill the body but cannot kill the soul. Rather fear him who can destroy both soul and body in hell" (Matthew 10:28). In context, Jesus is specifically addressing persecution. But the principle is that whatever the world finds most fearful in this temporal age is nothing compared to eternity in hell. Notice that Jesus doesn't say "fear going to hell separated from God." Hell is indeed separation from God's blessing, but it is, nevertheless, the presence of God's cursing. A biblical fear/peace paradigm requires a person's felt fears and perceived threats, valid as they might be, to subordinate under what the Bible teaches is supremely fearful: God's justice. That is bad news. Fear God.

---

8 Consider a few examples of this pattern in the Bible: Isaiah 53:5; Ephesians 2:14–18; Colossians 1:19–22.

On the cross, after a life of truly loving God and others in perfect obedience to God's law, Christ took on the law's curse so that all who trust in Him alone could take on the law's blessings. Of the drama of redemptive history, this was comedy, tragedy, and fairy tale all played out in one act, titled, as it were, "God's Great Exchange." Comedy, because God would love the objects of His wrath. Tragedy, because God would curse His truly pleasing Son in their place. Fairy tale, because God would impute His Son's righteousness to them and bestow on them all the blessings and privileges of the adopted sons of God. No guilt. No fear. That is good news. Peace with God.

Counterfeit Peace

All people seek rest in the peace that the world gives (government control, medical experts, retirement plans, insurance, security systems, etc.), and yet, their souls remain troubled. They have no peace. Unbelievers immersed in fear/peace cultural value systems find themselves pining over what comes next, seeking to practice whatever routines have "worked" in the past to ward off calamity, placate the spirits, and ensure stability. Moreover, living in fixation of fear has its corrosive effects. Over time people grow calloused to the threats, and mitigating those threats seems terribly draining. Resolution after resolution, routine after routine, year after year, the rat race never relents. So, in a burst of impulsiveness, they throw it all to the wind, so to speak, and live recklessly for the moment.

Their secret wish is that whatever comes next—the afterlife, reincarnation, rebirth—will prove better than this life. But they realize there is no guarantee that their next existence will improve. So, because their moral code remains intact, they dabble a bit with doing good to neighbor, honoring their parents, burning incense to their deceased ancestors, and avoiding any acutely wicked demerits like murder or betrayal. Then, lying in their bed in the hollow silence of the night, having depleted their dopamine high, with their smartphone battery dead and no access to anesthetizing entertainment, haunted by a troubled conscience, they concede that they will never be good enough. So, the cycle reboots: Fear. Ritual. Routine. Fade. Fail. Fornicate. Intoxicate. Regret. Fear. Repeat.

The thought of death worries Christians as well. We know our devotions, church attendance, parenting, internet searches, thought lives, spending habits, and fantasies are not good enough in preparation for meeting God. And what we fear is an index of what we love and value most. For instance, if our fear of chronic sickness and aging inordinately influences our thinking, spending, and lifestyle, then we reveal an inordinate love and value for health and youthfulness. And those inordinate loves become so heavy they crush us under their taxing demands. So, whatever our fears might be, Christians around the world pursue peace through spiritual experiences, mission trips, exercise and healthy eating, financial security, affirmation from pastors, association with Christian celebrities, and generally, seeking to do more. This is essentially legalism—seeking a peaceful assurance in one's ability to be good enough or avoid sin enough so as to obtain God's blessings. These fear-based tactics of achieving peace are merely twenty-first-century versions of medieval indulgences, fashioned to temporarily anesthetize fearful consciences.

Practical Applications

A Pre-Evangelism Conversation

Tenzin was a Tibetan Buddhist monk who invited me into his humble home and kindly showed me the Tibetan holy sites in his high-mountain village. [9]

---

9   For a corresponding conversation with Tenzin, see chapter 7 in Burns, Ancient Gospel, Brave New World.

Missionary: "Those temples are quite ornate. I find the architecture and features of these holy sites to be quite interesting. How often do you go to temple, and what do you do?"

Tenzin: "I go as often as I can. I recite the mantras, meditate, and perform the basic rituals of spinning the prayer wheels, lighting candles, prostrating, making offerings, and just trying to build merit. I'd really like to go on a pilgrimage someday. That would be extra good."

M: "What's the purpose of these rituals?"

T: "To get more merits and accumulate your karma. If we don't accrue enough karma through good acts and good thoughts, bad things inevitably happen. Do you remember that earthquake that destroyed my family's neighboring village? Everyone knows they had bad karma. There might have been one or two people with many secret demerits, but no one knows who for sure. So, everyone knows they each need to work harder at earning more righteousness."

M: "So, what's the end goal of getting enough merits?"

T: "I guess it's to achieve enlightenment and nirvana, but until then, I hope to be reborn into something better in the next cycle. Honestly, ever since I was a kid, I have always felt afraid of doing something bad and ruining my family or bringing terrible misfortune. Sometimes I feel like evil spirits torment me in the temple or the mountains and even in my dreams. But other times, when I think I have done enough merits, it seems like there are good spirits that help me not be so afraid. I am mostly worried about karmic retribution upon my family. We really just want our health, businesses, and herds to thrive and grow. Only a few times have I been righteous enough that I felt like I could have peace and harmony for a while. But that passed after a few days or a week."

M: "Who taught you about karma the most? How do you know it's true?"

T: "My father and mother, of course. I suppose I learned a lot in temple instruction as well. I don't know how it's true; it's just the way the world works. You get what you deserve. Don't you Christians say, 'You reap what you sow?'"

M: "Yes, you're right. Christians believe all sinners eventually get what they deserve. But how do you know when you have done enough good deeds and had enough pure thoughts?"

T: "I don't know. There's really no way to know. That's why we live in fear. The more we work out our merits, the more our minds are not actually at peace because we know we can never do enough. I just want to do enough."

A Simple Gospel Explanation

After the missionary has held numerous pre-evangelism con-versations and multiple occasions of teaching the doctrines of revelation, God, creation, sin, man, and Christ, they can follow up with this simple gospel explanation that pulls it all together. In many fear/peace value systems, developing first a doctrine of creation is paramount because their interpretation of reality is quite distinct from Christian doctrine. This is obviously a mere example, the details of which might not easily connect to all fear/peace paradigms:

> The Bible teaches that God has always existed and all that exists depends on Him. He created the world by speaking it into being. Because He rules the world by the word of His power, He has created the laws of nature. Nothing happens randomly apart from His will. Because of our first ancestor, Adam, we are truly bad. Adam's demerits passed on to all his family, so our problem is that we are all guilty like him.

We all suffer under the curse of breaking God's moral law. And there is none righteous, not even one. So, it's amazing that we experience anything good at all. Why do good things happen to unrighteous people? Because God, in His immeasurable benevolence, has granted us all a season of amnesty. This life we live is not to earn merits, but rather, it is an opportunity to turn from our demerits and trust in God's solution to our problem of unrighteousness. In the place of ill-deserving sinners, God sent Jesus to earth to live the perfectly righteous life we all should have lived but couldn't and to suffer the penalty of our demerits. God raised Him from the dead to conquer death, demons, and all that is fearful because of our bad deeds. Evil spirits, once harassing us because of our condemnation, no longer have dominion over those whom God covers with His favor. In forsaking our imperfect attempts at meriting righteousness and through trusting alone in Jesus's righteous life and death in our place, God will declare us truly righteous and grant us the peace of reconciliation with Him. This peaceful union with Christ on the ground of His righteousness is free, full, and forever. He gives us His Spirit to live inside of us as a temple, and His Spirit speaks peace to us and reminds us that we are safe and secure in God's family. The peace we can enjoy in God is as sure and steady as the eternal weight of Christ's merits and the retribution He satisfied for us. Even though we will still stumble and sin in this life, through faith alone our peaceful righteousness in Christ can never terminate or diminish. Furthermore, we can never improve it based on any good we do. So, as Christ's Spirit empowers us, we pursue righteous living no longer out of fear but out of admiration and gratitude to Christ. And for all eternity, we will enjoy praising Him for the glory of His grace.

Discipleship Applications

Once karma-background believers start their discipleship process, one common quality with which they describe their newfound

Spirit-indwelt life is *peace*. They often will use other descriptors like *joy*, *happiness*, and *gratitude*, but above all, they feel safe, secure, and at peace, hence their joy and gratitude. The enemy, the world, their non-Christian family, and their sin nature will try to rob them of their newfound peace. Doubts arise, assurance wavers, and they desperately need to remember God's unending love. Their habitual tendency will be to revert to ritual and routine to avoid any demonic or karmic retribution for what they perceive has displeased God.

First, let us remind them that the Bible says, "There is no fear in love, but perfect love casts out fear. For fear has to do with punishment, and whoever fears has not been perfected in love" (1 John 4:18). Nevertheless, this does not mean that "the fear of the Lord" was for Old Testament worship, nor should we apply biblical fear as mere "congenial respect." Fear means fear. But in fearing God with godly fear, we then discover the joy of resting in His love—that the holy omnipotence that makes Him so ferociously fearful will never be used *against* us but always *for* us in Christ. The Holy Spirit in the Psalms says, "The friendship of the Lord is for those who fear him" (Psalm 25:14). Since God's perfect love casts out fear, which ultimately makes way for His perfect peace, then the battle against unwarranted fear starts with not doing just enough or doing more than enough. The battle starts with remembering and resting in God's justifying love for us in the work of Christ. We can never improve on God's love for us, and we can never detract from His love for us. The Father delights in us, His adopted righteous sons, as He delights in His only begotten righteous Son. His love is infinite (without measure), immutable (never changing), and eternal (without beginning or end) because He Himself is these things in His essence. A god whose love is more for some and less for others, whose love fluctuates, and whose love is temporal is a false god. But our God can love us no more, and He will love us no less.

Second, a glorious passage with which to calm an anxious soul comes from Jesus's lips: "Peace I leave with you; my peace I give to you. Not as the world gives do I give to you. Let not your hearts be troubled, neither let them be afraid" (John 14:27). Jesus promises peace, His peace. This is not some sort of ethereal, puerile, positive-thinking peace. This is true, heavenly peace. Jesus contrasts it with the peace that the world gives, which often looks like access to state-of-the-art medical care, equitable law enforcement, retirement savings, yogic tranquility, and an enjoyable job. But the peace that Christ offers transcends the priorities and felt needs of this life. When the doctor apologizes for not finding the terminal cancer earlier, when the once placated evils spirits trouble you at night, when the police fine you for a parking infraction but refuse to investigate your latest home burglary, when the economy crashes one month before your retirement, and when you have to wake up another day to do the job you hate for the boss who despises you, the worldly peace degenerates into worldly fear. Jesus later says, "I have said these things to you, that in me you may have peace. In the world you will have tribulation. But take heart; I have overcome the world" (John 16:33). The Bible says, "The peace of God, which surpasses all understanding, will guard your hearts and your minds in Christ Jesus" (Philippians 4:7). This divine peace that Christ promises us does not fall apart when the world falls apart, when the mountains crumble into the heart of the sea. The source of this peace is the transcendent God, and its experience is otherworldly.

Consider a meager sampling of Scripture's ample supply of peace-giving verses, in addition to the abovementioned, that bring hope to those who live in fear/peace cultural paradigms:

- And the effect of righteousness will be peace, and the result of righteousness, quietness and trust forever. My people will abide in a peaceful habitation, in secure dwellings, and in quiet resting places. (Isaiah 32:17–18)

- You keep him in perfect peace whose mind is stayed on you, because he trusts in you. Trust in the Lord forever, for the Lord God is an everlasting rock. (Isaiah 26:3–4)

- He who dwells in the shelter of the Most High will abide in the shadow of the Almighty. I will say to the Lord, "My refuge and my fortress, my God, in whom I trust." (Psalm 91:1–2)

- Even though I walk through the valley of the shadow of death, I will fear no evil,for you are with me; your rod and your staff, they comfort me. (Psalm 23:4)

- Blessed is the man who trusts in the Lord, whose trust is the Lord. He is like a tree planted by water, that sends out its roots by the stream, and does not fear when heat comes, for its leaves remain green, and is not anxious in the year of drought, for it does not cease to bear fruit. (Jeremiah 17:7–8)

- The Lord is on my side; I will not fear. What can man do to me? (Psalm 118:6)

- O Lord, you will ordain peace for us, for you have indeed done for us all our works. (Isaiah 26:12)

- Behold, I am with you always, to the end of the age. (Matthew 28:20)

Bringing It to Center

Christians and non-Christians alike struggle in fear/peace paradigms. To be sure, billions of unreached people perish under the crushing heaviness of their unrighteousness. Tormented by evil spirits, they know they can never do enough. Even Christians sometimes struggle with our own version of karmic Christianity, constantly trying to maintain God's favor and blessing through obedience, church activity, abstaining from bad habits, and overall busyness for God. On the cross, by Christ's obedient substitution, God exchanged our distressing guilt and dreadful curse for Christ's impeccable righteousness and blessings of *shalom*. On the cross, the immutable love of God and faithfulness of Christ established righteousness for a guilty people plagued by fear and the curse. The gospel of peace in Christ, grounded in His righteousness, received through resting in Him alone, is good news for self-justifying unbelievers and believers alike.

> Let me hear what God the Lord will speak,
> for he will speak peace to his people, to his saints;
> but let them not turn back to folly.
> Surely his salvation is near to those who fear him,
> that glory may dwell in our land.
> Steadfast love and faithfulness meet;
> righteousness and peace kiss each other.
> Faithfulness springs up from the ground,
> and righteousness looks down from the sky.
> Yes, the Lord will give what is good,
> and our land will yield its increase.
> Righteousness will go before him
> and make his footsteps a way.
>
> – Psalm 85:8–13

CHAPTER 5

Christ
Our Freedom

What cultural tendency frequently describes classic American Western movies? Some might say *grit*, while others might suggest *lawlessness*. Yet, those common descriptors fall beneath the larger tendency of "rugged individualism." What made the American West and, before that, oceanic exploration, so appealing to resilient individuals? Could it be that the unanticipated isolation, rootlessness, and transience forced a hardened self-reliance on otherwise community-oriented people who were willing to take a risk and "go West"?

Cultures of individualistic orientations are in some ways quite easy to identify. Individualism is a unique orientation that doesn't come easily to some because it seems counterintuitive to the community-oriented relational nature in all of us. For those whose family lineage has remained intact in one town for hundreds of years and who have never moved or lived internationally, their security is in the family, not in a college education or a career. But places that host much voluntary mobility and impermanence tend to be palpably individualistic. Consider the rich and upwardly mobile executives in Bangkok and Mumbai.

They might be only one generation removed from communal farm life in a remote village, but their functional orientation now operates like other urban professionals in most "concrete jungles"—self-sufficient, self-promoting, and self-pleasing. Indeed, high-powered businessmen in Vancouver, Seoul, São Paulo, and Dubai have more in common as functional individualists than with their own relatives laboring in secluded, communal agrarian towns.

Most individualistic cultures consist in the West generally and in the United States specifically. This is a true observation and quite obvious to most people who have used social media, watched American movies, and studied European and American history. In the secular West, erotic liberty has become a preeminent good of personal freedom. This is not the only expression of personal freedom, but it is by far the most marketed, ubiquitous, politicized, and addictive. Moreover, erotic liberty is so indelibly connected to the perceived personhood and emotional stability of each individual that to label eroticism as a lifestyle choice is to supposedly assault the well-being of the persons themselves.

The orientation and popularized tendency toward individualism generally emerged from French Enlightenment thinking of the seventeenth to nineteenth centuries. Now it is the popular culture marketed globally by incessant media campaigns, preying on easily distracted, narcissistic digital natives. Though it might seem that individualism is chiefly a Western construct, in today's globalized world, the "selfie generation" is increasingly self-oriented and consequently individualistic, yet not in the same way as the stereotypical Euro-American expression.

Some missiologists assume that guilt/innocence is the primary value system that corresponds to Western individualism. However, this is theologically incorrect, as we have reviewed, because the paradigm of guilt/righteousness originates from the Old and New

Testaments and corresponds to the original sin problem and God-given moral code in each culture. The guilt/righteousness paradigm is not a phenomenon of the Enlightenment. Additionally, it seems more historically and socially accurate to conclude that the touchstone of Western individualism is the lust for liberty, self-sufficiency, and personal autonomy. The Enlightenment unleashed the autonomous self that our globalized Western culture so cultishly celebrates. The devotion to the individual self and the antipathy for external constraint and restriction find their roots in the minds of the intellectuals and philosophers of humanism. This is not to say that *individuality* is a humanistic, secularist concoction. *Individualism* is not *individuality*. Misunderstandings abound when conflating individualism with individual responsibility. The former is humanistic, and the latter is Judeo-Christian. Likewise, individualism and collectivism are godless perversions of the virtuous expressions of individuality and community.

The cohesive orientation of radical individualism is godless secularism, though that does not necessarily precipitate atheistic secularism. Secular society certainly has its committed atheists, but more widespread than atheism is a secular mysticism. This blends New Age "enlightenment," horoscopes, and mindfulness with a self-defined pantheism that all serve the narcissistic journey of self-discovery and individual liberation. The perceived original sin problem in radical individualism is external realities, traditions, systemic injustices, and identities forced on a person. Its corresponding felt "sin" is a constraint to be and do what authorities require, feeling oppressed in a reality of which you are a victim, and feeling stuck in an unhappy life. The salvation for an individualist is liberation from the societal constructs, life-consequences, and enslaving ideas of whatever makes them feel like a prisoner. And the pursuit of growth in that salvation system is self-discovery, self-liberation, self-expression, and self-celebration. Compelling others to likewise celebrate one's liberated individualism is the logical endgame of hyper-individualism. To be sure, not all people of an individualistic orientation are equally radical, but they all share in measure the same cultural value paradigm: bondage/freedom.

The bondage/freedom paradigm influences and expands from the other cultural value paradigms, like the fear/peace paradigm. Nonetheless, it is predominant in an individualistic orientation. As aforementioned, individualism—the unfettered pursuit of unbiblical individual autonomy—is not the same as individual responsibility and accountability, which Scripture certainly teaches. Much of the implications of the original sin problem manifest themselves in the sinner's quest for godlikeness and freedom from God's law. Throughout the Bible, descriptions of sin use such language. People who see life through the lens of bondage/freedom tend to experience the objective reality of their guilt in a broad range of emotions, but most commonly they might describe their plight as "stuck" or "trapped." Yet because their self-made identity revolves around their bondage, they aren't always forthright about their regrets because that would erode their reputation of being brave and liberated. But they are slaves to their self-made freedom.

The Gospel for Bondage/Freedom Value Systems

Scripture is replete with the paradigm of bondage/freedom, employing synonymous ideas like slavery/redemption, servitude/ deliverance, and even death/life. This paradigm can sometimes blend naturally with a fear/peace paradigm and even a weakness/ strength paradigm. It is not a static, standalone construct. Yet it is distinct enough that it deserves to be theologically unpacked. The natural instinct that we are all in bondage is common to the human experience and operative moral code. It is unmistakable even in the created order: "For the creation waits with eager longing for the revealing of the sons of God. For the creation was subjected to futility, not willingly, but because of him who subjected it, in hope that the creation itself will be set free from its bondage to corruption and obtain the freedom of the glory of the children of God" (Romans 8:19–21). Under the curse, every birth has its death, every love story has its heartache, every parent has their regret, every majestic volcano has its devastating eruption, and every technological breakthrough fades into obsolescence. Eternity is in our hearts, and we groan for the freedom of Eden.

God made man to be a worshiper, and in bondage to sin, the human heart creates its own gods to serve (Romans 1:18–25). Those gods are typically whatever man trusts to be the source of his perceived freedom. And peddlers of those gods always provide a code to follow, a wage to merit, a condition to meet. No religious or political system provides freedom for nothing. Even transferring citizenship from a war-ravaged country to a

> **Bondage/Freedom Value System Terms**
>
> Slavery. Constraint. Restraint. Control. Chains. Shackles. Stuck. Suppression. Obligation. Tradition. Oppression. External. Servitude. Consequence. Authoritarian. Liberty. Self-Love. Self-Discovery. Self-Expression. Autonomy. Independence. Choice. Self-Celebration. Self-Sufficiency. Rights. Entitlement.

sanctuary country requires following steps, passing tests, waiting in line, and obeying the law. The bridge that spans the chasm between slavery and freedom is law. No one merely walks out of prison without paying their due, and no one merely walks across a national border and receives citizenship without following the lawful prerequisites. So it is in every religious system and cultural value paradigm. People want to be free, so they do what makes them feel free.

Faith Alone for Bondage/Freedom

True freedom in Christ is not merely freedom from the law's demands and penalty, nor is it even freedom merely to enjoy all the benefits of being a Christian. But freedom in Christ is freedom *to rest in Christ*, abide in Christ, love Christ, and belong to Christ. It is not only freedom *from* God's law and penalty but freedom *for* God's love and pleasure. The problem of the sinful heart is that its desires enslave it, and the heart always chooses according to its strongest desire (John 8:44; 1 Thessalonians 4:5). In Christ, those desires are finally set free to love God according to God's good design for His people. No one's will is truly free until their will is set free from its bondage to sin and made right with God. Paul argues, "It was for freedom that Christ set us free; therefore keep standing firm and do not be subject again to a yoke of slavery" (Galatians 5:1, NASB).

No longer fearing damnation under God's law, we can now resist the domination of sin and therefore love God and experience freedom in Christ to enjoy the Father's good pleasure, the very *telos* for which He created us. This is what it means to have a truly free will. From the law's demands and God's judgment on our guilt, God set us free *in Christ* to be free *to Christ* and *for Christ*. Just as Eve was from Adam, for Adam, brought to Adam, and named by Adam, so Christ rejoices over His redeemed Bride: "I have called you by name; you are mine" (Isaiah 43:1–7; see also 62:2–5).

Guilt/Righteousness for Bondage/Freedom

It is a glorious thing that we are not ascetics and need not worry about afflicting our bodies and depriving ourselves of normal, creational enjoyments for the sake of "self-made religion" (Colossians 2:16–23). Scripture argues that such severity to the body and ascetic practices are regulations (laws) that accord "to human precepts and teachings" (Colossians 2:22). Sadly, Christians fall back into rules and laws to achieve freedom from sin, "but they are of no value in stopping the indulgence of the flesh" (Colossians 2:23). A sinister form of Christianized gnosticism exists in every era. Christianized gnosticism borrows man-made laws (regulations, principles, teachings) because they guarantee spiritual insight, personal improvement, and escape from the trappings of the flesh.

The Holy Spirit through Paul establishes these imperatives about avoiding man-made laws and gnostic religion in the redemptive indicatives of the preceding verses:

> And you, who were dead in your trespasses and the uncircumcision of your flesh, God made alive together with him, having forgiven us all our trespasses, by canceling the record of debt that stood against us with its legal demands. This he set aside, nailing it to the cross. He disarmed the rulers and authorities and put them to open shame, by triumphing over them in him. (Colossians 2:13–15)

These are the gospel truths that give the basis for the commands to not give in to man-made rules that promise freedom from the flesh. The Holy Spirit through Paul shows how freedom in Christ indissolubly emanates from His substitutionary cross-work that annulled our guilt with all its legal demands.

Moreover, as an example of how cultural orientations and cultural value systems exist on a spectrum, fear/peace and bondage/freedom paradigms overlap, especially in these issues of demonic doctrines. Because so many man-made gnostic rules and codes are demonic in origin, believers can rest assured that in the act of dealing a deathblow to our guilt and legal debt, Christ conquered the demonic rulers and authorities and publicly humiliated them. He proved them to be powerless without a legal basis for the prosecution of His people. The law and its legal demands over us were the rulers' bludgeon to hold us as prisoners. But now that Christ's substitutionary atonement has canceled our guilt and we are alive together with Christ, demonic spirits no longer have dominion over us. No accusation can stick.

Earlier in Colossians, it says, "He has delivered us from the domain of darkness and transferred us to the kingdom of his beloved Son, in whom we have redemption, the forgiveness of sins" (Colossians 1:13–14). Freedom in Christ is not just freedom from the dominion of darkness; it is freedom to be always *in* Christ. Union with Him. Clothed in His righteousness. Alive in Him. Hidden with Him. God never looks at us again with angry vengeance. His demeanor toward us is love—the enjoyment He has for His perfectly obedient Son.

God has imputed to us—orphaned by sin and enslaved to its dominion and damnation—His Son's righteousness, legally adopting us into His household. We are His. He is ours. Where justification is the *forensic* basis that fixes our guilt problem and makes us pleasing in God's eyes, adoption is the *filial* blessing that welcomes us into the loving presence of the Father. It will never to be rescinded or threatened. Indeed, justification is the foundational reality of our freedom *in* Christ, and adoption is the supreme enjoyment of our freedom in Christ *for* the Father.[10]

The Great Exchange

Christ took on the form of a slave, humbling Himself to death, even death on an inglorious cross (Philippians 2:7–8) so that He might credit His freedom to those enslaved to death's dominion. He was forsaken in order that those orphaned by sin might be adopted into the freedom of the Father. Exchanging His right standing with God the Father, Jesus made us not only right with

---

10   Consider a few examples of this pattern in the Bible: Romans 6:6–11; 8:1–4, 15–17.

the Judge but pleasing to His Father. Taking on the law's damnation and death's dominion, Jesus merited freedom and favor for us.

The freedom produced by the imputation of Christ's righteousness is a life in the loving favor of our adoptive Father. God imputes to us this freedom, which leads to devotion and loyalty to the Father. But never do we attain this freedom through our devotion and loyalty. That's law. And God gave the law to show how trapped we were in bondage to sin and death. Christ fulfilled this law for us and then gives us credit for what He did. "But when the fullness of time had come, God sent forth his Son, born of a woman, born under the law, to redeem those who were under the law, so that we might receive adoption as sons" (Galatians 4:4–5).

Counterfeit Freedom

The world offers a false freedom that never satisfies. The world's population spends billions of dollars each year to experience something thrilling and transfixing that gives them an escapist surge of freedom. Whether or not they are individualists, people want to be free. And the pursuit of freedom in diverse cultures might appear different, but at its root, it is a human longing. The modern world seeks freedom through such things as liberation from external responsibility and authority, mind-altering ecstasy, sexual expressiveness, and self-discovery. Many are the world's false freedoms that we chase after in hope of what only Christ offers.

Where the gospel is planted and grows in the world, often many counterfeit gospels infest the good soil. The Holy Spirit through Paul warns that there were "false brothers secretly brought in—who slipped in to spy out our freedom that we have in Christ Jesus, so that they might bring us into slavery"

(Galatians 2:4). We would all do well to heed the Holy Spirit's warning through Paul: "Now I urge you, brethren, keep your eye on those who cause dissensions and hindrances contrary to the teaching which you learned, and turn away from them. For such men are slaves, not of our Lord Christ but of their own appetites; and by their smooth and flattering speech they deceive the hearts of the unsuspecting" (Romans 16:17–18, NASB95).

Especially in remote areas of the world among karma-background believers, false teachers peddle seemingly innocuous rules and regulations for maintaining and ensuring God's pleasure and blessing. Sure, the young believers might rejoice that their sins are forgiven at conversion or baptism, but what about all those secret sins they still struggle with as Christians? Their financial hardship, cancer diagnosis, motorbike crash, or untimely death of a loved one all must be God's retribution for their ongoing struggle with a secret sin or their lukewarm devotional life, so they presume. Then they subconsciously revert to their anesthetizing karmic behavior of ritual, routine, and good deeds. Yet this time their cycle of merits takes on a Christianized façade: volunteer at church more, post prayer times on social media, give more money to the itinerant prophet, sing more sincerely, pray louder, fast longer, share the gospel more than anyone else at church, and require strict obedience of their children. In other words, get busy for Jesus. Then the freedom of God's blessings will incrementally come. But they describe it as "allegiance, loyalty, surrender, and reckless abandon to Christ's kingship."

The irony is that such a karmic system is not freedom at all. It might feel exhilarating at first—the adrenaline rush of extraordinary sacrifice or fresh resolve to greater devotion. But in the end, the dopamine high wears off, the intensity wanes, and our noble self-imposed expectations remain unmet. And once again, we fail to add up. Though truly well-intentioned, such efforts can quickly move from glad-hearted service to guilt-induced servitude. Law. Bondage.

Practical Applications

A Pre-Evangelism Conversation

Jaimie was a male prostitute in Chicago, one of many to whom I had been explaining the gospel while I worked for an urban outreach.[11]

Missionary: "Are you originally from here? Tell me what brought you to this neighborhood in Chicago?"

Jaimie: "Uh, well, I don't have any family. My roots are in Miami, but my home is wherever I want it to be."

M: "Is Chicago a good fit for you? Do you feel like you belong here?"

J: "I like Chicago for now because I can be whatever I want. I got friends. Chicago's a big *@!#% city, and I like how I can get lost in the hustle. If I don't like what I do, I do something else. No one's gonna tell me what to do."

M: "What do you do for a living?"

J: "&*$%!, I sleep around. I got my sex change, and let me tell you, there's big money for queer folk like me. You'd be surprised how much rich guys from the suburbs and even politicians will pay for me. I can get dope, pay rent, buy cutsie clothes, and eat good food with that cash."

M: "What made you want to make that transition? How long ago was that?"

J: "About three to four years ago. I wanted to because I was gay, and I felt a little trapped in that label. I still like guys,

---

11 For a corresponding conversation with Jaimie, see chapter 8 in Burns, *Ancient Gospel, Brave New World.*

but I've always wanted to be a chick. I wanted to be different and show off my inner self. I'm fabulous. I guess I just didn't care anymore about what others thought. We all deserve to be free."

M: "What do you think most people want to be free from?"

J: "I don't know. I guess we all know there are things about ourselves we don't like, and some stuff we just can't do enough to fix. We're kind of stuck. So, some people snort coke, others drink, and I got a sex change. I think we're all running from something, and we just do whatever it takes to get away."

M: "How do you know we're all stuck? What's the problem?"

J: "I remember feeling like I could never do enough good things to make my life work out the way I wanted. I got tired of trying to be the good kid for nothing. So I finally said, '%$!*# it.' I know we all do bad things, but we gotta think positive to get out of this mess we're living in. People everywhere just wanna be free."

M: "How do you know this? Why do you believe it?"

A Simple Gospel Explanation

For people in these types of contexts, many pre-evangelism conversations of asking penetrating questions are usually necessary. Once the missionary has a chance to explain the doctrines of revelation, God, creation, sin, man, and Christ, below is a simple gospel explanation that seeks to interact with the felt burdens of feeling trapped and the felt needs of freedom. Using this value system to lead into explaining the central point of God's grace in Christ's atonement and righteousness can have its challenges. One challenge is that some people in individualistic orientations are familiar with Christianity because of Christian cultural influence. They might have heard of Jesus, the cross, sin, and other

Christian language. Carefully explaining what you mean and don't mean is critical. Also, leading into a gospel explanation with their value system in mind, one will quickly see that hyper-individualists and pleasure-seekers often tie their personal identity to their lifestyle. It can carry a lot of emotion. Thus, any comments that chastise their lifestyle will shut them down, and they won't listen. Here is an example of how to briefly put together a gospel explanation after laying a basic foundation of gospel doctrine:

> The Bible teaches that God has created all things for good purposes, including you and me. Yet, His ways are not our ways. Part of His design for humans was to know Him and enjoy Him. The Bible tells us that Adam did what was right in his own eyes and sinned against God. This act condemned all Adam's descendants as guilty, and like Adam, we all do what is right in our own eyes. We make decisions based on our sinful nature. But there's something about our sinful nature that doesn't satisfy us. Deep down inside, we know we were designed for something better and more enjoyable. But as it is, we feel stuck, trapped in a cycle of trying the next best thing. Something is wrong with us, and we don't know how to fix it. The problem is that we are guilty and under the curse. But our hearts long to be free in the blessings for which God initially created Adam and the rest of us. Therefore, since God is rich in mercy, He sent Jesus to live the perfect life according to God's rules and earn righteousness for us. And Jesus took away our captivity to sin in His death and substituted Himself for us so that through trusting in Him alone, we can be counted as truly righteous before God. But when our chains of sin are broken off and we are united to Christ through faith alone, we can enjoy the freedom to know God and enjoy Him forever. All our seeking to escape feeling trapped and our pursuing elusive freedom in this life can only be fulfilled by turning away from trying to do enough and by resting in Christ alone for forgiveness, righteousness, and adoption into God's family.

Discipleship Applications

In my limited experience and observation, which is not exhaustive by any means, Christians around the world speak of freedom in Christ typically in terms of freedom to enjoy things that other Christians might find offensive or in terms of freedom to be more expressive and emotive in prayer and singing in public worship. It seems that freedom in Christ takes on a whole new hue when we see it through the lens of justification that leads to adoption, legal acceptance, and loving approval. The sweet doctrine of adoption is unspeakably life-giving to those who cower under fear of God's perpetual displeasure, especially for those who come out of a karmic system. They feel like they can never keep up with the motivational pep talks they hear on Sunday and the moral exactitude they impose on their own children. Deep down inside, they know their best is never just enough. And once again, on the 31st of December, at 11:59 p.m., as they hope for a better New Year, regret and guilt haunt their reflections like bad dreams. They feel stuck. In bondage. Hopefully, they'll do better and be good enough next year. As for the freedom of resting in Christ? It's too good to be true. Midnight. The cycle reboots.

Be careful not to leave them only with steps for better obedience. Though in many cases, young believers and first-generation believers of historically unreached ethnolinguistic groups truly need to know the Bible's practical teaching on holy living. But this should be done in the context of a consistent rehearsal of justification and adoption. This requires the teacher and disciple-maker to plan ahead and frequently reinforce these doctrines. No one gets it merely through osmosis, as it were. The biblical gospel is categorically *other*. How could it not be since its source is the special revelation of the transcendent God? No cultural value system or cultural orientation compares. And so, competence to teach the full counsel of God is critical.

Moreover, distinguishing sonship language as part of our freed status as righteous in Christ is quite illuminating. To be a son was to be the exclusive heir of the father's reputation and inheritance. Daughters never inherited such status. They were indeed cherished, but they never enjoyed the rights and privileges of being a son. So, sonship language is a massive promotion (not demotion) for women or children, slave or free, Jew or Gentile. It is neither sexist nor old-fashioned. To receive treatment as a son is to be the most privileged and esteemed heir. The richness of the doctrine of adoption demands sonship language. We are not merely God's children—we are His sons, His heirs.

Furthermore, when orphans receive adoption, they never resemble the adoptive father. In a sense, they are always different. Conversely, when God the Father adopts sinners as sons, He begins the sanctifying work of conforming us into the image of His begotten Son, who is the image of the invisible God. The Father not only frees us from condemnation (justification) and frees us out of our corruption to sin (sanctification) but He also sets us free into conformity to the image and likeness of Jesus (glorification). We resemble Him.

In teaching and disciple-making, we should acknowledge that all of us groan inwardly for final freedom from sin forever. But we should also be careful not to confuse our inward groan for resurrection with God's perceived irritation for our imperfect allegiance to Him. In addition to the previous passages, here are some wonderful texts to expound, all from Romans 8:

- For the anxious longing of the creation waits eagerly for the revealing of the sons of God. For the creation was subjected to futility, not willingly, but because of Him who subjected it, in hope that the creation itself also will be set free from its slavery to corruption into the freedom of the glory of the children of God. For we know that the whole creation groans and suffers the pains of childbirth together until now. And not only this, but also we ourselves, having the first fruits of the Spirit, even we ourselves groan within ourselves, waiting eagerly for our adoption as sons, the redemption of our body. (Romans 8:19–23 NASB95)

- And we know that God causes all things to work together for good to those who love God, to those who are called according to His purpose. For those whom He foreknew, He also predestined to become conformed to the image of His Son, so that He would be the firstborn among many brethren; and these whom He predestined, He also called; and these whom He called, He also justified; and these whom He justified, He also glorified. (Romans 8:28–30 NASB95)

- He who did not spare His own Son, but delivered Him over for us all, how will He not also with Him freely give us all things? (Romans 8:32 NASB95)

Bringing It to Center

All these gospel truths we have reviewed are lavish with the glory of God's grace. Presenting these truths about freedom in Christ on the ground of His substitutionary atonement and righteousness is awesome to those in bondage to the never-ending pursuit of freedom. For those who can never do enough or find enough freedom, the imputation of righteousness and adoption into God's family is spectacularly good news. Abiding in and meditating on these truths can win the hearts and affections of believers to rest in Christ's righteousness and the freedom of the Father's immutable love. Let us all rest in the freedom of the love of God in Christ, that He has adopted us through substitution.

Therefore let it be known to you, brethren, that through Him forgiveness of sins is proclaimed to you, and through Him everyone who believes is freed from all things, from which you could not be freed through the Law of Moses.
– Acts 13:38–39 NASB95

CHAPTER 6

Christ
Our Strength

Have you read a novel or seen a movie that portrays a belligerent preacher who seems to browbeat people into heaven? Think of popular accounts of old-fashioned revivalists and fire-and-brimstone preachers. Aside from scaring the Hades out of people, what do you imagine them chastising? Often we associate their jeremiads with warnings against the world's pleasures and delights. Whether or not such stereotypes are historically accurate, when Christians think of materialism, we often think of the love of the world's goods—worldliness, idolatry. And yet in secular philosophy, materialism can mean the antithesis of idealism—focusing on the mind and consciousness. Using the word *materialism* in these ways is not wrong. But for our purposes here, on the continuum of cultural orientations, just as individualism and collectivism are polar opposites, materialism and spiritualism are also at opposite ends of the cultural spectrum. Paradoxically, places in the world that appear to be the most spiritualistic can be surprisingly materialistic. How does that make sense?

Many people assume that a cultural value paradigm of weakness/strength or poverty/power starkly belongs in a spiritualistic orientation and not a materialistic one. And, indeed, that was also my assumption for years until I started listening to indigenous Christian leaders in contexts typically categorized as spiritualistic or animistic. Even still, as discussed previously, animistic/spiritualistic peoples undeniably exist in some areas of the world, and their experiences with demons, karmic fears, and demonic retribution absolutely riddle them with anxiety. As we saw, though they unquestionably gravitate toward power, they *primarily* long for the final product of power—peace and safety.

But cultural contexts that blend spiritualism and animism (e.g., parts of Africa, Latin America, and South Asia) sometimes have a deeper dilemma. The battle they fight on a regular basis is not so much conscious demonic oppression and possession, though that sadly happens too often. Their biggest daily obstacles center on the insurmountable plight of powerlessness, poverty, weakness, vulnerability, instability, and disadvantage. People plagued by poverty and weakness tend to turn to forms of power, be it in miracle workers, political leaders, the wealthy, or even the charitable. The reason is that they all seem to guarantee upward mobility, wealth, health, and strength to climb out of life's pits.

Though some philosophers and missiologists might disagree, it seems that the shared, day-to-day, hour-by-hour conscious burden of the average person in a destitute context mainly entails general powerlessness and the heaviness and despair of poverty (and by that, I mean an inability or lack of opportunity to create life-improving wholeness and capital). They indeed might integrate the spiritual dimension to their proposed solutions but as a means to a physical, material end. When the spiritual is integrated, it's not mainly because it is objectively true but usually because it seems to work and is perceived as *useful* for their felt needs. Of course, no one knows the heart, but observationally, this utilitarian emphasis seems to be quite common.

The challenge here is not establishing equality of outcome but equality of opportunity. Truly, some people suffer demonization, and I have witnessed cases of demonic oppression and possession. It is tragic and distressing. Yet, for most people, fighting disappointment and hardship due to helplessness is their daily and hourly challenge, not fighting the fear of demonic manifestations. For missionaries and ministers serving in these contexts, addressing the deeper realities below the felt needs and perceived ultimate threats is quite precarious to navigate. Satan is a master at counterfeit distractions that divert attention from the indicatives of the gospel to the implications of the gospel.

The Gospel for Weakness/Strength Value Systems

In the Sermon on the Mount, we easily miss the fact that Jesus was doing a few things: He was revealing the holy perfection the law has always required by showing that the Torah since the beginning has meticulously judged the heart's intentions and the mind's thoughts (Matthew 5:22–48). The law is not merely ten steps to a closer walk with God. The law reveals God's perfect will for the community in covenant relationship with Him—truly loving Him and truly loving one another. Jesus came to fulfill the law, not abolish it (Matthew 5:17), and to dispense the covenant's blessings to His people, weak and helpless to love God and others perfectly (1 Peter 1:16; Leviticus 11:44).

That His people are united to Him by trust alone and thus receive the imputation of His obedience is the foundation of His blessings to His people. The Sermon on the Mount is good news in that it shows to what extent the Messiah would fulfill the law and the prophets for His trusting people. He's the Righteous One that the Old Testament had always been awaiting (John 5:46). The required righteousness that exceeded that of the scribes and Pharisees (Matthew 5:20) is qualitatively distinct. Despite all the Pharisees' devotion to law-keeping, they still fell short of God's holy standard. What is His standard? Perfection equal to God the Father (Matthew 5:48). The good news is that credit for this perfect standard is ours as a gracious gift, which we receive through trust in Christ alone.

Therefore, in the Beatitudes, Jesus revealed Himself as the better Moses, the better covenant Mediator. He is the kingdom come. He comes as the Priest-King to His own mount, one of grace, to bestow the blessings of the covenant and the kingdom. Thematically, this relates to Jesus's announcement of His earthly mission (which should not be confused with marching orders for the church): "The Spirit of the Lord is upon me, because he has anointed me to proclaim good news to the poor. He has sent me to proclaim liberty to the captives and recovering of sight to the blind, to set at liberty those who are oppressed, to proclaim the year of the Lord's favor" (Luke 4:18–19).

In the Beatitudes, no imperatives exist. He does not command, "Be poor, and you will be blessed; be meek, and you shall inherit the earth; be merciful, and you will receive mercy, etc." The indicatives of the Beatitudes are pronouncements of covenant blessings on those humble who look to the Messiah in their weakness to save them despite the Pharisees' teachings. Then come instructions for keeping the letter and spirit of the law and the consequent covenant curses for those who reject the Messiah by seeking God's commendation in their own strength (Matthew 5:21ff). The epistles then interpret Christ's actions as the covenant King coming to bestow grace and blessings on His spiritually impoverished people who, in solidarity, are united to Him through trust alone.

Upon receiving these gracious blessings in Christ, believers seek to walk in grace and gratitude. The Sermon on the Mount, then, becomes indicative of kingdom living for Spirit-filled, Spirit-empowered saints who are already credited with perfect righteousness. Jesus's teachings throughout Matthew become *useful* for kingdom living (though never perfectly attained in this life) for the blessed ones who already have His indwelling Spirit and His empowering work in this new covenant age.

Faith Alone for Weakness/Strength

The felt needs of weakness—infirmity, helplessness, vulnerability, poverty—are not illegitimate. They correspond to the human condition. God genuinely cares about the world's needs, so He causes it to rain on the just and the unjust. He is a benevolent Creator and Sustainer. Whether or not people turn to Christ in the kindness of God (Romans 2:4), God will nonetheless show divine magnanimity and equity to mankind. That does not mean He will never send earthquakes or plagues or any other calamity, and it does not mean God is not wrathful or will someday universally save all people. But affectionately ministering to a person's most concentrated locus of conscious suffering—HIV, abuse, trauma, mental illness, poverty-related disease, extortion, fatherlessness—is a good deed done for love of neighbor in imitation of Christ. Yet, the more loving act would be to help weak, suffering people understand the saving love of God in Christ.

Many chronically suffering people interpret much of life through a cultural value system of weakness and strength. Acknowledging their felt needs and validating their struggles are not only humane but Christlike. Moreover, unpacking how the groanings of their temporal suffering correspond to the eternal problem of the curse and Adamic guilt is truly loving and just. And forgiveness and justification through trust in Christ's work alone secure for us a new life that will experience its ultimate cure in the resurrection.

Until that great day, God has sent the Spirit as our Helper to make us more like Christ in preparation to reign with Him in the resurrection. And whether God has ordained to heal us in this life of our varied weaknesses and afflictions, Christ remains the strength of our life. Countless are the biblical promises of God carrying His people through weakness, weariness, and tribulation safely home to glory.

In Scripture, trust in God corresponds to a humble, thankful heart that receives divine strength. Trust does not pretend there are no threats or dangers assailing and wearying the Christian. Pride, rather, presumes that the Christian is able, strong, and experienced enough to walk independently of relying on God. The self-confident Christian, though, would never admit this in such terms. But a lifestyle of prayerlessness, thanklessness, and self-assuredness is indicative of a haughty spirit. And the root of a prideful and haughty spirit is unbelief, or distrust.

An abiding trust in God does not guarantee a life free of infirmity, weakness, and demonic opposition. Hardly. In fact, a trusting heart that rests on God will likely suffer regular attacks from demonic spirits. However, trust in God abides in His very present help and strength, confident in His past redeeming grace and expectant of heavenly glory. Trust humbly confesses a need for help and waits on God to make good on His promises. Pride, rather, is self-assured and boastful.

We see how trust in God's power strengthens and prepares God's people for eschatological glory. Paul prayed thus for the church in Colossae:

> Be filled with the knowledge of his will in all spiritual wisdom and understanding, so as to walk in a manner worthy of the Lord, fully pleasing to him, bearing fruit in every good work and increasing in the knowledge of God; being strengthened with all power, according to

his glorious might, for all endurance and patience with joy; giving thanks to the Father, who has qualified you to share in the inheritance of the saints in light. He has delivered us from the domain of darkness and transferred us to the kingdom of his beloved Son, in whom we have redemption, the forgiveness of sins. (Colossians 1:9–14)

Here the Holy Spirit through Paul uses three synonyms of God's ability—*strengthened*, *power*, and *might*—to enable His saints to live in a way that is worthy of Him, pleasing, fruitful, and characterized by endurance, patience, joy, and thankfulness. And all this because the Father has powerfully delivered the saints from darkness into the inheritance of the kingdom of Christ. God's awesome power opens the door to our inheritance in His beloved Son's kingdom, which emanates from the Son's redeeming work—the forgiveness of sins.

Guilt/Righteousness for Weakness/Strength

Anywhere in the world that has access to a smartphone—which is nearly everywhere now—the globalized marketing agenda has triumphed. We are a self-referential and self-loving generation, caring more about our projected image and self-made identity on social media than the legitimate needs of others in our immediate presence. With such an obtuse infatuation with the tyranny of the "now," we have diminished the awareness of the eternal. Voyeurism has replaced vigilance.

> **Weakness/Strength Value System Terms**
>
> Poverty. Poor. Infirmity. Frailty. Vulnerability. Recovery. Authority. Disadvantage. Difficulty. Burden. Hardship. Affliction. Brokenhearted. Healing. Sorrowful. Forsaken. Restoration. Distress. Disease. Powerlessness. Helplessness. Guard. Protection. Defense. Compassion. Power. Force. Might. Mercy. Joy. Help. Advantage. Ability. Capacity. Prosperity. Success. Health. Wealth.

The body image has eclipsed the soul. And the body is merely a hodgepodge of body parts for the objectification of the nearest self-indulgent pervert. In the pornographization of personhood, we have forgotten that we are eternity-bound embodied souls, not glandular animals running wild in heat.

Consequently, the human experience of the globalized twenty-first century is one of insidious, narcissistic fragility and a commensurate loss of courage, duty, virtue, wisdom, and beauty. The perceived problems are brokenness, self-dissatisfaction, oppression, and rejection. The perceived solutions, then, are wholeness, self-acceptance, the overturning of oppressive systems, and being liked. So, the gurus of our modern age hawk never-ending steps and man-made rules that guarantee happiness, wellness, acceptance, virility, and recognition.

Just as we must define terms in other cultural value systems, we must do the same for people whose value system centers on weakness/strength because therapeutic jargon, victimhood ideology, and oppressed/oppressor language pervade the post-truth psyche. We must not assume they understand biblical definitions of the similar-sounding vocabulary we might use. The problem is not that they feel bad about themselves and can never do enough to "arrive" at real happiness or human flourishing. The true problem, rather, is that God is angry at guilty sinners and will punish them for eternity unless they trust in Jesus's blood and righteousness and turn from their rebellion. Deep down inside, they know something is profoundly broken in the human experience. And though their moral code drives them to try something new, try harder, and act more confident, the curse corrupts and ruins everything. But new life in Christ will turn the groanings they feel into joy, strength, and faith.

Yet, lest we confuse the abundant-life benefits of flourishing under the reign of Christ with knowing Christ Himself through the gospel, we must highlight the original sin problem as it corresponds to their felt needs. And then we must announce the solution found in Christ's cross-work and resurrection. They need to understand that the root problem is they are guilty before God and that Jesus's atoning death and righteousness can remedy their guilt problem.[12]

The Great Exchange

Though afflicted and wounded by sin, "with his wounds we are healed" (Isaiah 53:5)—Christ's wounds exchanged for our healing. Our ungodly weakness and sinful powerlessness to ascend the hill of the Lord and stand in His holy place (Psalms 15; 24:3–4) find their remedy in the justifying death of Christ. Christ suffered and endured the penalty of sin in our place as our Substitute, exchanging with us His righteousness for our unrighteousness. This was all to powerfully achieve what our sin and Adamic guilt weakened us from ever accomplishing: access to God Himself. "Therefore, since we have been justified by faith, we have peace with God through our Lord Jesus Christ. Through him we have also obtained access by faith into this grace in which we stand" (Romans 5:1–2). The Holy Spirit through Peter says, "For Christ also suffered once for sins, the righteous for the unrighteous, that he might bring us to God, being put to death in the flesh but made alive in the spirit" (1 Peter 3:18).

As Gentiles, we were hopeless and helpless without God's promises. But Christ was our scapegoat, expiating our guilt, that we might be brought near to God: "Remember that you were at that time separated from Christ, alienated from the commonwealth of Israel and strangers to the covenants of promise, having no hope and without God in the world. But now in Christ Jesus you who once were far off have been brough near by the blood of Christ" (Ephesians 2:12–13).

---

12   Consider a few examples of this pattern in the Bible: Psalm 79:8–9; Isaiah 64:6–7; Jeremiah 33:6–8.

Counterfeit Strength

The world has mastered the shtick of selling people false strength. False strength is in the superhero movies that captivate people with stories of tremendous might and killer instinct. Counterfeit power manifests itself in our most precious idols—political command, business savvy, cultural influence, firearms, muscle cars, sexual manipulation, and unrivaled wealth. You can take away a man's money and a man's woman, but don't touch his control. Control is the drug of choice of this world. It is an idol of the heart that consumes and ruins more than most, which is why absolute power corrupts absolutely. It is probably the most god-like experience a person can have.

Counterfeit power and control even exist among Christians. Some contemporary Christian scholarship and popular trends assume a mandate for the church to participate in God's agenda to transform culture, redeem society, improve the environment, reverse climate change, ensure social justice, and finish the revolution of love launched by Christ. Many of these ideas are noble "Christian" alternatives of worldly elitist sensibilities and altruistic priorities. These essentially comprise a "secular theology"—a subset of liberation theology—that claims the church's mission is to improve the world and take its agenda from the world.

It is true that the Christian can indeed hope for blessings of ultimate horizontal equity and reconciliation. Yet these benefits and implications of the gospel will fully manifest in the resurrection. The full blessings of what Christ will bring to fulfillment in the resurrection are not imperatives for Christians to accomplish in this present evil age. As increasingly more sinners repent and trust in Christ, the blessings of the gospel will permeate social structures, but this only in degree and as a mere foretaste of the resurrection. The heart of the gospel for sinners in this age is that we have objective vertical reconciliation with God now because Jesus became our propitiation and satisfied God's justice.

Many Christians among the world's urban poor, migrant workers, factory laborers, and village farmers work long hours every day, Sunday through Saturday, just to eat and acquire basic necessities. Such impoverished Christians' greatest concern is not the transformation of society. They struggle with heavy discouragement, infirmity, weakness, and a pervasive sense of helplessness. They have no insurance and no workers' compensation. Their workplace injuries corrode their well-being and jeopardize their livelihood. They view life through the value system of weakness and strength, poverty and power. Their hope is not in a better life now. Their hope is in the return of Christ, the beatific vision. And in that hope, they rejoice and find the strength to endure another day. What makes them love to honor their King is that He is their Savior who is coming back to finally deliver them.

Practical Applications

Duong was a leper who lived in a remote leper colony in the jungles of Vietnam.[13] I had been traveling and ministering with a Vietnamese pastor, and one time when visiting Duong, I learned from the pastor about a pre-evangelism conversation that influenced Duong's conversion to Christ.

A Pre-Evangelism Conversation

Missionary: "How long have you been living in this village, Duong? Where are you from?"

Duong: "I don't know. A long time. My family couldn't take care of me, and many of our neighbors were afraid of my sickness. They dropped me off somewhere on the road, and then I got brought here. I don't remember everything that

---

13   For a corresponding conversation with Duong, see chapter 9 in Burns, Ancient Gospel, Brave New World.

happened. Oh, by the way, you don't need to be afraid of me. I don't think I will get you sick."

M: "What you have had to endure is so sad. I am quite sorry to hear that. Would you mind telling me about your sickness and when that started?"

D: "I don't remember when it all started, but basically, I don't have feeling. And since I don't have feeling, I accidentally hurt myself. And my wounds look scary to people. See my hand? I lost my three fingers because I caught them on fire, but because it didn't hurt, I didn't put them out quickly enough. One time I realized that I was chewing up my tongue and not meat. So that's why I talk funny. I had a lot of problems, and the nearby monks would come to my village and tell my family they could restore me. But my family had to make offerings to them first. After paying so much money and getting no healing over time, I think my family had to give up."

M: "You don't need to say anymore. I'm sure this is hard to talk about. What do you hope to get here at the leper colony?"

D: "The problem was that my family could never do enough to fix my disability. They were spending all their money to pay the monks, and nothing was working. My mother had to leave and find a factory job in Ho Chi Minh [City] just to make some more money. Now that I'm here, I want to get better. Maybe I can get a job here sweeping the floor and send money home. But I can hardly walk straight or use my hands, so I don't know. I need help, but I also think it's wrong not to help my family."

M: "What do you think your family needs most?"

D: "They need money. My father has done drugs too, so I think we lost money from that. My sister then went to work at a massage parlor. And I don't think that's good. We all have problems, but if we think positive enough and do good enough, we can be strong."

M: "Why do you think that? How do you know?"

A Simple Gospel Explanation

In light of a weakness/strength cultural value system, slowly teach the redemptive framework for the Bible and God's purposes. And after explaining the core doctrines of revelation, God, creation, man, sin, and Christ, one can use this simple gospel explanation that could bring it all together:

The Bible teaches that God is the God who sees. He is all-seeing. He knows where you struggle, those unheard groans and dark feelings of despair. The Bible tells us He created all things good but that Adam did wrong by not following God's rules. Because Adam betrayed God, the consequence of Adam's guilt was a curse on all his descendants and all creation. We are all guilty in Adam and under the curse. Nothing is as it should be, and deep down inside, we know it. Every birth has its death, every marriage has its disappointment, every harvest has its toil and labor. As hard as we try, we can never do enough to reverse the brokenness we feel in this life. And some of us suffer more than others. We don't know why, but if we are honest with ourselves, sometimes we think it's our fault. Something is wrong with us. Whether our struggles are truly our fault—since not all infirmities are direct results of something we did—nevertheless, there is indeed something wrong with us. We are weak but not *mainly* weak in the way that we perceive. Our physical and material weakness points to our spiritual weakness. The problem is that there is none righteous, not even one. But God, in His rich mercy, sent Jesus to become weak that we might be strong. Jesus was wounded that we might be healed, and He lived the righteous life according to God's law that we could not and would not live. He suffered the penalty our guilt deserved. God raised Jesus from the dead to new life to secure righteousness for us and give us the power of His Holy Spirit. Jesus knows how to sympathize with our weakness, and He is powerful to save us from the curse and even eternal death. God will someday raise us from the dead, and we will enjoy all the powerful blessings of being counted righteous in Christ. All this can be ours freely through only trusting in Christ alone. We can add nothing to His power on our behalf. This is all to the praise of the glory of the grace of God, the very purpose for which He created us.

Discipleship Applications

For Christians deep in the milieu of a weakness/strength cultural paradigm, sometimes temptations exist to use biblical verses as proof texts for steps to victorious living, success, self-confidence, and material blessing. In making disciples in these contexts of those who struggle with ongoing weakness and who wonder at the promises of God for help, it helps to remember that God sent a thorn to the apostle Paul. God did this to keep him from boasting in his own strength and becoming conceited for his special revelatory privileges. He was an apostle whom God granted the power to heal on occasions, but even after Paul pleaded with God three times to remove his thorn in the flesh (and these were likely extended seasons of prayer), God's answer seemed counterintuitive. But it was not inconsistent with how God helps His people in this life: "But he said to me, 'My grace is sufficient for you, for my power is made perfect in weakness.' Therefore I will boast all the more gladly of my weaknesses, so that the power of Christ may rest upon me. For the sake of Christ, then, I am content with weaknesses, insults, hardships, persecutions, and calamities. For when I am weak, then I am strong" (2 Corinthians 12:9–10). God's discipline for Christians is never punitive but always purifying.

Reminding those we are discipling about the Holy Spirit's power working through us is of great importance. The temptation is to think that God only helps those who really try hard or who are truly sincere or desperate enough. But the Spirit's empowering work is much freer and more constant than we might realize.

The Holy Spirit through the apostles teaches us that the life we live in Christ is empowered by Christ to the glory of Christ: "For this I toil, struggling with all his energy that he powerfully works within me" (Colossians 1:29), and "But by the grace of God I am what I am, and his grace toward me was not in vain. On the contrary, I worked harder than any of them, though it was not I, but the grace of God that is with me" (1 Corinthians 15:10), and "Whoever serves, as one who serves by the strength that God supplies—in order that in everything God may be glorified through Jesus Christ" (1 Peter 4:11).

In other words, we must underline that we ourselves are powerless to contribute anything pleasing to God. But Christ's power in us enables us through resting in Him to do what can only be explained by the power of resurrection life breaking through our weakness. And this is so that He gets all the attention and credit for any fruit from our lives. Therefore, any blessing and rewards for fruitful obedience are strictly rewards of grace. In our experience of fruit-bearing, to extend the metaphor, the sun, the rain, the root, the sap, the branches, and the fruit are all gifts of God's grace in Christ. This is the power of the life of Christ in us. It doesn't mean we don't spend ourselves out of love for God and others. It just means that we rest in Jesus's righteousness and thus work gratefully with all His might that powerfully works in us. These concepts are essential for us to remember.

The Bible is replete with promises that God will uphold and sustain His weary people. And Christians operating in weakness/strength paradigms struggle every day. For those seeking to make disciples in this context, this paradigm differs significantly from other shame, fear, and bondage contexts. Someone might indeed struggle with shame, fear, and bondage quite regularly, but often those feelings might dissipate for a while through distractions, relationships, work, and anesthetizing behaviors. But with weakness, because it often attaches to something tangible and physical (e.g., low-caste pariahs, chronic fatigue, joblessness, impairment, chronic pain, psychosis, addiction, homelessness, mental trauma), the incessant consciousness of suffering plagues the person's mind without mercy. This is where the grace and compassion of God are so vast and inexhaustible that the weary soul must draw near with full assurance, trusting in the good designs of our heavenly Father. Though we might feel like sheep led to the slaughter (Romans 8:36), no evil will finally befall those who trust in Jesus. In other words, suffering and weakness are common human experiences under the curse, but for the Christian, this is our worst life now. The best is always yet to come. God is infinite, and we are not. So, for all eternity, discovering and enjoying the love of the triune God will only increase in intensity, day after day, century after century. Ten million years from now in the marvelous presence of God, the best is still yet to come.

For many vulnerable Christians, promises of short-term physical and material blessings based on man-made rules seem alluring and doable. Consequently, the cycle of merits to earn God's blessing starts. In teaching and disciple-making in a predominant weakness/strength value paradigm, we must remind our brothers and sisters that resurrection power does not promise deliverance *from* hardship in this life. Rather, Christ's resurrection power in us delivers us *through* hardship and will deliver us finally in the next life.

Sometimes we receive glimpses of our future resurrection when God graciously bestows healing. But the normal Christian life is trusting in God to be enough for us in Christ, relying on Him who raises the dead: "Indeed, we felt that we had received the sentence of death. But that was to make us rely not on ourselves but on God who raises the dead" (2 Corinthians 1:9). Below are a few wonderful verses from the massive amount of promises to struggling believers that God is enough for us in times of trial and hardship:

- Come to me, all who labor and are heavy laden, and I will give you rest. Take my yoke upon you, and learn from me, for I am gentle and lowly in heart, and you will find rest for your souls. For my yoke is easy, and my burden is light. (Matthew 11:28–30)

- Have you not known? Have you not heard? The LORD is the everlasting God, the Creator of the ends of the earth. He does not faint or grow weary; His understanding is unsearchable. He gives power to the faint, and to him who has no might he increases strength. Even youths shall faint and be weary, and young men shall fall exhausted; but they who wait for the LORD shall renew their strength; they shall mount up with wings like eagles; they shall run and not be weary; they shall walk and not faint. (Isaiah 40:28–31)

- A bruised reed he will not break, and a faintly burning wick he will not quench; he will faithfully bring forth justice. He will not grow faint or be discouraged till he has established justice in the earth. (Isaiah 42:3–4)

- Thus says the LORD: "Let not the wise man boast in his wisdom, let not the mighty man boast in his might, let not the rich man boast in his riches, but let him who boasts boast in this, that he understand and knows me, that I am the LORD who practices steadfast love, justice, and righteousness in the earth. For in these things I delight, declares the LORD." (Jeremiah 9:23–24)

- The LORD is near to the brokenhearted and saves the crushed in spirit. (Psalm 34:18)

- Whom have I in heaven but you? And there is nothing on earth that I desire besides you. My flesh and my heart may fail, but God is the strength of my heart and my portion forever. (Psalm 73:25–26)

Bringing It to Center

God loves to powerfully save impoverished souls languishing in darkness. The Lord is good and gracious to help His struggling children. He is mighty to deliver His children through unremitting suffering and poverty of soul. The saint who trusts in Jesus for forgiveness and righteousness and rests in His sovereign care knows the secret of being content. Glad-hearted contentment and restfulness in God are indicative of a saint who knows the power of Christ's resurrection life. The resurrection is our great hope. The power of the resurrection in this life is not a guarantee of total deliverance *from* suffering. Rather, it is the power to persevere *through* suffering, looking to Jesus, the Author and Perfector of our faith.

> For the word of the cross is folly to those who are perishing, but to us who are being saved it is the power of God. . . . For the foolishness of God is wiser than men, and the weakness of God is stronger than men. For consider your calling, brothers: not many of you were wise according to worldly standards, not many were powerful, not many were of noble birth. But God chose what is foolish in the world to shame the wise; God chose what is weak in the world to shame the strong; God chose what is low and despised in the world, even things that are not, to bring to nothing things that are, so that no human being might boast in the presence of God. And because of him you are in Christ Jesus, who became to us wisdom from God, righteousness and sanctification and redemption, so that, as it is written, "Let the one who boasts, boast in the Lord."
>
> – 1 Corinthians 1:18, 25–31

"As One of the King's Sons"

The biblical gospel neither adapts nor adopts the imperfect meaning of the world's value systems. Rather, with transcendent truth, the Bible reinterprets and fills up biblically defined *honor*, *peace*, *freedom*, and *strength*. It brings clarity to them in the light of the lordship of Christ. The transcultural Word of God brings cohesion and meaning to those cultural value systems by showing how the benefits/blessings of Christ's work depend on the redemptive center of His work: penal substitutionary atonement, the imputation of His righteousness, adoption into His family, reconciliation with God, and union with Him in his death and resurrection.

Many cultures value honor, peace, freedom, and strength, and the way the world achieves them requires doing enough according to a common code. But Christian doctrine teaches that Christ's substitutionary work is enough to secure such blessings and benefits. They are benefits of the gospel that God bestows freely on the legal ground of Christ's imputed righteousness. And so, united to Christ through faith alone, we receive Christ and all that He is for us—infinite, immutable, and eternal honor, peace, freedom, and strength. God's ways are not man's ways.

The centrality of a guilt/righteousness paradigm is the standard key to unlocking the gospel for the world's macro-cultural value paradigms of shame/honor, fear/peace, bondage/freedom, and weakness/strength. Trust alone receives Christ Himself and His benefits and blessings secured by His righteousness and atonement. Those gospel benefits and blessings are the true substance of the patterns of God's image valued in some cultural orientations. The exchanges of Christ's righteousness and His benefits and blessings for our unrighteousness and curses depend on His substitution and imputation.

A Concluding Gospel Study: Mephibosheth

This book has introduced a handful of characters, all representing people I have known in multiple contexts around the world. Imagine a gospel teaching (for oral-based learners) with Jaimie, Duong, Tenzin, and Abdul all present—each viewing life through their cultural orientation and each trying in vain to do and be enough according to their blend of value systems. In this illustration, the assumption is that they have received teaching about the basic doctrinal categories necessary to make sense of the gospel. This elaborated analogy rehearses the biblical narrative of David and Mephibosheth from 2 Samuel 4–9 to illustrate God's saving grace for us in Christ. Its main point will highlight the truth that God welcomes weak, fearful, shameful, and enslaved sinners to receive His grace and rest in union with Christ. After the missionary explains how the stories of the Old Testament can serve as analogies and shadows of the coming Messiah, they can relate the narrative below, the basic content of this lesson adapted and expanded to support the purposes of this book:

> Have you ever felt trapped in a situation or a reality from which you could not escape? Maybe you have suffered weakness or hardship that seemed irreversible. Maybe people were ashamed and embarrassed by you because of something

you couldn't remedy. Have you ever longed to merely have simple peace? It's not that you demand something extraordinary, but you just wish you could make it all better. The burden you carry is ruthless, and it seems that no matter what you do, it is never enough. These are all common echoes and consequences of the curse on mankind. The fundamental problem is that our first ancestor, Adam, sinned against God and did what was right in his own eyes. Since then, his family line has received his guilt and corrupt nature. Our guilt renders us unable, and our corruption makes us unwilling to live righteously before God. So, our burden is tenacious, and we can never do enough.

Let me introduce a young man who languished under a great burden. His name was Mephibosheth; he lived during the reign of King David of Israel. The book of 2 Samuel records his life, and he first arrives on the scene in 2 Samuel 4. Mephibosheth was the young son of Jonathan, David's best friend. Jonathan's father was Saul, who was the king that had hunted down David to kill him. Both Saul and Jonathan died in battle with the Philistines near the Jezreel Valley. As was the custom, when a ruler died in battle, often his family would also be killed to prevent the royal line from claiming the throne. The woman who was caring for the five-year-old Mephibosheth heard the news and fled with him in her arms and dropped him. His fall paralyzed his legs. Just a day before, this active young boy was likely playing innocently with friends, wondering when his father would return and confidently resting in the reality that he was an heir in the royal family. In one moment, all that changed. The blessings of strength, honor, peace, and freedom came crashing down. He was now trapped in his new identity as an orphan, an enemy of King David's line, and a cripple.

In the meantime, 2 Samuel 7 details that Yahweh gave David rest from all his enemies. David wanted to then build a house for Yahweh. But Yahweh said He would build His house through another king. Yahweh made a covenant with David, which we call the Davidic covenant, that from David's royal line would come an Anointed King who would rule an eternal kingdom. This great and gracious promise from

Yahweh caused David to worship and fear Him for His ill-deserved kindness.

In 2 Samuel 9, David asks if there was anyone left alive in Saul's family. Now, any normal king would be asking that question in order to eliminate all opposition and vindicate the name of the new reign. Bloodlines ran deep in the ancient world. Loyalty to family name was everything. But David's intent was to "show the kindness of God" to a descendant of Saul (2 Samuel 9:3). The unmerited kindness of Yahweh to David so captivated him that he likewise wanted to share Yahweh's kindness to others. David's servants went to summon Mephibosheth, who was living in Lo-debar, which meant "land of nothing," a forsaken land.

Mephibosheth was likely trembling with anxiety. Since his accident, he had been a burden to everyone around him. People needed to help dress, bathe, move, and do everything for him. He had no father to provide for him nor protect him. He'd repeatedly heard that he was a shameful, infirmed orphan who was on the king's hit list. He was guilty because of Saul, his family head. It was just a matter of time before Mephibosheth got what was coming to him. Anxiously awake at night, in pain, mourning his father, and scared that the king's soldiers might find him, Mephibosheth knew he was a disgrace and a liability to all those around him. He knew he could never do enough to get out of his trouble and appease the king.

Then one day, the king's servant found him and quickly delivered him to the king. Upon entering the king's presence, Mephibosheth fell on his face in fear. Mephibosheth had nothing to offer to the king. David called him by name, "Mephibosheth!" and graciously spoke: "Do not fear, for I will show you kindness for the sake of your father Jonathan, and I will restore to you all the land of Saul your father, and you shall eat at my table always" (2 Samuel 9:6, 7). The only thing Mephibosheth could do was receive David's irresistible kindness and trust him to fulfill his promises.

Any debts and punishment that burdened Mephibosheth became expiated in that moment. Mephibosheth received the declaration of being in the right with the king. No longer was he condemned. David treated him as his own royal son. And David instructed his servants to make sure Saul's land was tilled and harvested and that Mephibosheth always had plenty to eat.

David's status was forensically imputed to Mephibosheth, and from his legal adopted position as a son of the king, Mephibosheth enjoyed the filial blessings and benefits of honor, peace, freedom, and strength. Out of his shame, he received honor. His unremitting fear gave way to secure *shalom*. He was finally free from bondage to Saul's name and all its trappings. And in his weakness and infirmity, he was strong, well-fed, and well supplied. It was everything he had ever desired and more. David's grace and kindness were more than enough for him. And the best part of it all? Mephibosheth got to enjoy his adoptive father, King David, every day: "Mephibosheth ate at David's table as one of the king's sons" (2 Samuel 9:11 NASB). David seated Mephibosheth at his table to be with him.

The lead character of this story is not Mephibosheth, nor is it David, though David is indeed a hero and a wonderful example of compassion. Yahweh, however, is the true protagonist, who first bestowed covenantal kindness on David. And in response to Yahweh's kindness, David adopted Mephibosheth. The analogy of David's redemptive grace seems to prefigure *the* Hero from his lineage: Jesus is the better King David who "receives sinners and eats with them" (Luke 15:1–2).

Bringing It to Center

Jesus is the true King, and that is good news. Moreover, *the* good news is that this King wielded His sovereign power to save sinners by obediently fulfilling all the demands of God's law. "For the LORD is our judge, the LORD is our lawgiver, the LORD is our king; He will save us" (Isaiah 33:22 NASB). As our Substitute, He absorbed the curses of the covenant and secured its spiritual blessings for those upon whom His grace rests—those who turn from their unrighteousness and trust alone in Christ alone. After taking our just penalty on the cross and then rising from the dead in resurrection glory, Jesus stands alive as the better King David. This better King freely imputes righteousness to sinners orphaned, crippled, disgraced, and trembling in bondage to Adamic guilt. In union with Christ, on the basis of His work of propitiation and justification, we receive God's Holy Spirit to live in the freedom of the glory of the children of God. We are saved by God, from God, because of God, and for God. And that is more than enough for a sinful world.

> *But God, being rich in mercy, because of the great love with which He loved us, even when we were dead in our trespasses, made us alive together with Christ—by grace you have been saved—and raised us up with Him and seated us with Him in the heavenly places in Christ Jesus, so that in the coming ages He might show the immeasurable riches of His grace in kindness toward us in Christ Jesus. For by grace you have been saved through faith. And this is not your own doing; it is the gift of God, not a result of works, so that no one may boast.*
>
> – Ephesians 2:4–9

The Transcultural Gospel Model

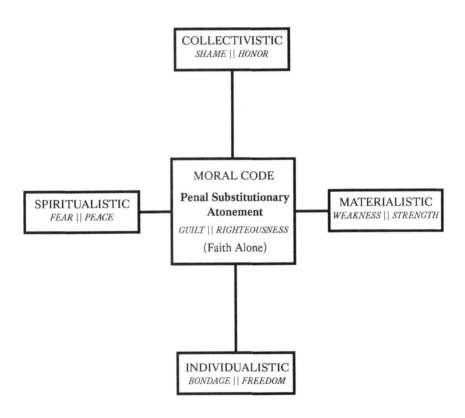

The Transcultural Gospel Model
and
Overlapping Cultural Value Systems

FEAR/PEACE
- Anxiety
- Karma
- Calamity
- Wholeness
- Stability
- Assurance

SHAME/ HONOR
- Defilement
- Disapproval
- Abandonment
- Belonging
- Clean
- Reputation

Guilt/ Righteousness

BONDAGE/ FREEDOM
- Constraint
- Oppression
- Servitude
- Liberty
- Autonomy
- Independence

WEAKNESS/ STRENGTH
- Poor
- Helpless
- Unable
- Power
- Endurance
- Able

Scripture Index

Old Testament

Genesis

3:6	23, 49
3:10	23, 49
6:8	62

Leviticus

11:44	91
19:18	46
20:17–19	49

Deuteronomy

6:5	46

2 Samuel

9:3	110
9:6-7	110
9:11	111

Psalms

15	97
23:4	71
24:3-4	97
25:14	55, 69
34:18	105
73:25–26	105
79:8–9	97n1
85:8–13	72
91:1–2	71
118:6	71

Psalms (cont)

119:130	26
130:4	54

Isaiah

6:2	61
24:14–16	42
26:3–4	71
26:12	71
32:17–18	70
33:22	111
40:28–31	105
42:3	54
42:3–4	105
43:1–7	78
45:20–22	39
53:5	97
55:6–7	55
62:2–5	78
64:6–7	97n1

Jeremiah

9:23–24	105
17:7–8	71
33:6–8	97n1

New Testament

Other Titles from Founders Press

BY WHAT STANDARD? God's World... God's Rules.
Edited by Jared Longshore

I'm grateful for the courage of these men and the clarity of their voices. This is a vitally important volume, sounding all the right notes of passion, warning, instruction, and hope.

—Phil Johnson, Executive Director of Grace To You

Truth & Grace Memory Books
Edited by Thomas K. Ascol

Memorizing a good, age-appropriate catechism is as valuable for learning the Bible as memorizing multiplication tables is for learning mathematics.

—Dr. Don Whitney, Professor,
The Southern Baptist Theological Seminary

Dear Timothy: Letters on Pastoral Ministry
Edited by Thomas K. Ascol

Get this book. So many experienced pastors have written in this book it is a gold mine of wisdom for young pastors in how to preach and carry out their ministerial life.

—Joel Beeke, President,
Puritan Reformed Theological Seminary

The Mystery of Christ, His Covenant & His Kingdom
By Samuel Renihan

This book serves for an excellent and rich primer on covenant theology and demonstrates how it leads from the Covenant of Redemption to the final claiming and purifying of the people given by the Father to the Son.

—Tom Nettles, Retired Professor of Historical Theology,
The Southern Baptist Theological Seminary

Strong And Courageous: Following Jesus Amid the Rise of America's New Religion

By Tom Ascol and Jared Longshore

> We have had quite enough of "Be Nice and Inoffensive." We are overflowing with "Be Tolerant and Sensitive." It is high time that we were admonished to "Be Strong and Courageous."'

—Jim Scott Orrick, Author,
Pastor of Bullitt Lick Baptist Church

Additional titles

Wisdom for Kings & Queens: Truth for Life from the Book of Proverbs
By Jared Longshore

Still Confessing: An Exposition of the Baptist Faith & Message 2000
By Daniel Scheiderer

By His Grace and for His Glory
By Tom Nettles

Getting the Garden Right
By Richard C. Barcellos

The Law and the Gospel
By Ernie Reisinger

Teaching Truth, Training Hearts
By Tom Nettles

Coming in 2021

Praise Is His Gracious Choice:
Corporate Worship Expressing Biblical Truth
By Dr. Tom Nettles

Just Thinking: About the State
By Darrell Harrison and Virgil Walker

Ancient Gospel, Brave New World
By E.D. Burns

Galatians: He Did It All
By Baruch Maoz

Missions by the Book
By Chad Vegas and Alex Kocman

Baptist Symbolics Vol. 1
For the Vindication of the Truth: A Brief Exposition of the
First London Baptist Confession of Faith
By James M. Renihan

Order these titles and more at press.founders.org